Good Housekeeping

Favourite
Quick &
Easy Meals

250 Tried, tested, trusted recipes ★ Delicious results

Good Housekeeping

Favourite
Quick &
Easy Meals

250 Tried, tested, trusted recipes ★ Delicious results

COLLINS & BROWN

First published in the United Kingdom in 2010 by
Collins & Brown
10 Southcombe Street
London
W14 0RA

An imprint of Anova Books Company Ltd

The Good Housekeeping website is
www.allaboutyou.com/goodhousekeeping

10 9 8 7 6 5 4 3 2 1

ISBN 978-1-84340-589-4
A catalogue record for this book is available from the
British Library.

Reproduction by Dot Gradations UK Ltd
Printed and bound by Times Offset Malaysia

This book can be ordered direct from the publisher at
www.anovabooks.com

Recipes in this book are taken from the Good Housekeeping recipe
library and may have been reproduced in previous publications.

Picture Credits:
Neil Barclay (pages 18, 23, 58, 79, 84, 85, 90, 98, 106, 108, 109,
111, 146, 186 and 204); Martin Brigdale (pages 124, 128, 129,
147, 148, 153, 154, 163, 179, 182, 188, 192, 197, 210, 216,
218, 219, 222, 226, 249, 271 and 272); Nicki Dowey (pages 10,
11, 12, 13, 14, 15, 16, 17, 19, 20, 21, 22, 25, 26, 27, 28, 30, 31,
32, 33, 36, 38, 39, 41, 43, 44, 45, 46, 47, 48, 50, 53, 54, 55,
56, 57, 63, 66, 69, 71, 72, 73, 74, 80, 81, 82, 86, 92, 93, 94,
95, 100, 101, 103, 105, 107, 110, 114, 117, 118, 126, 132,
133, 134, 136, 140, 141, 143, 144, 145, 149, 151, 156, 157,
160, 161, 162, 164, 167, 168, 169, 171, 172, 173, 174, 175,
177, 180, 184, 185, 187, 190, 191, 193, 196, 198, 199, 202,
207, 209, 211, 217, 220, 221, 223, 224, 227, 228, 229, 230,
236, 237, 238, 239, 240, 241, 242, 243, 245, 246, 247, 250,
251, 252, 253, 254, 255, 258, 259, 261, 264, 267, 274, 280,
281, 282 and 283); Will Heap (pages 29, 62, 135, 178, 203, 231
and 262); Craig Robertson (pages 24, 40, 51, 52, 60, 65, 75, 78,
83, 87, 88, 89, 91, 99, 102, 112, 113, 115, 119, 120, 122, 127,
137, 139, 142, 150, 152, 155, 165, 175, 183, 189, 195, 205,
206, 214, 221, 233, 248, 260, 263, 265, 266, 268, 269, 270,
273, 275, 276, 277, 278, 279, 284 and 285); Lucinda Symons
(pages 37, 49, 59, 64, 67, 68, 70, 116, 123, 170, 194, 208, 213
and 232)
Home Economists: Anna Burges-Lumsden, Joanna Farrow, Emma
Jane Frost, Teresa Goldfinch, Alice Hart, Lucy McKelvie, Mari
Mererid Williams, Kim Morphew, Katie Rogers, Bridget Sargeson
and Jennifer White
Stylists: Susannah Blake, Wei Tang, Helen Trent and Fanny Ward

NOTES

- ★ Both metric and imperial measures are given for the recipes. Follow either set of measures, not a mixture of both, as they are not interchangeable.
- ★ All spoon measures are level.
  1 tsp = 5ml spoon; 1 tbsp = 15ml spoon.
- ★ Ovens and grills must be preheated to the specified temperature.
- ★ Medium eggs should be used except where otherwise specified.

DIETARY GUIDELINES

- ★ Note that certain recipes contain raw or lightly cooked eggs. The young, elderly, pregnant women and anyone with immune-deficiency disease should avoid these because of the slight risk of salmonella.
- ★ Note that some recipes contain alcohol. Check the ingredients list before serving to children.

Contents

Foreword

I love food that's bursting with flavour – but I know that recipes with long lists of ingredients are immediately off-putting to busy people. After all, who's got time to wade through complicated instructions, then traipse around shops desperately searching for obscure ingredients? And not to mention spending hours slaving over a hot stove…

Don't get me wrong, gourmet meals are great for weekend entertaining, or if you are catering for a special occasion, but what we all really want is practical mid-week eating solutions. You want to feed your family and yourself well, but realise that time isn't always on your side in the kitchen. This is why this fantastic cookbook will become your saviour – quick, easy and practical meals, with no compromise on flavour.

In the time it takes you to heat up a ready meal or dial for a takeaway, you can have a fresh, home-cooked meal on the table – it really is that quick. Home-cooking will also ensure that you are in complete control of your nutritional intake, which can only be a good thing.

Each recipe in this book has been triple-tested for taste and reliability. The reputation of Good Housekeeping means you can relax when you get cooking, as you have a guarantee that the recipes will work and taste wonderful.

Read on and be inspired…

Meike.

Meike Beck
Chief Home Economist

Start the Day ★

Porridge with Dried Fruit

Preparation Time 5 minutes • Cooking Time 5 minutes • Serves 4 • Per Serving 279 calories, 6g fat (of which 1g saturates), 49g carbohydrate, 0.2g salt • Vegetarian • Easy

200g (7oz) porridge oats
400ml (14fl oz) milk, plus extra
  to serve
75g (3oz) mixture of chopped dried
  figs, apricots and raisins

1 Put the oats into a large pan and add the milk and 400ml (14fl oz) water. Stir in the figs, apricots and raisins and heat gently, stirring until the porridge thickens and the oats are cooked.

2 Divide among four bowls and serve with a splash of milk.

Toasted Oats with Berries

Preparation Time 10 minutes, plus cooling • Cooking Time 5–10 minutes • Serves 4 • Per Serving 327 calories, 15g fat (of which 3g saturates), 44g carbohydrate, 0.1g salt • Vegetarian • Easy

25g (1oz) hazelnuts, roughly
  chopped
125g (4oz) rolled oats
1 tbsp olive oil
125g (4oz) strawberries, sliced
250g (9oz) blueberries
200g (7oz) Greek yogurt
2 tbsp runny honey

1 Preheat the grill to medium. Put the hazelnuts into a bowl with the oats. Drizzle with the oil and mix well, then spread out on a baking sheet. Toast the oat mixture for 5–10 minutes until it starts to crisp up. Remove from the heat and set aside to cool.

2 Put the strawberries into a large bowl with the blueberries and yogurt. Stir in the oats and hazelnuts, drizzle with the honey and divide among four dishes. Serve immediately.

⭐ COOK'S TIP
Blueberries contain a substance that helps the gut to stay clean and healthy, and, like cranberries, they are rich in antioxidants.

⭐ TRY SOMETHING DIFFERENT
Use a mixture of raspberries, blackberries, or chopped nectarines or peaches instead of the strawberries and blueberries.

Energy-boosting Muesli

Preparation Time 5 minutes • Makes 15 servings • Per Serving 208 calories, 9g fat (of which trace saturates), 28g carbohydrate, 0g salt • Vegetarian • Dairy Free • Easy

500g (1lb 2oz) porridge oats
100g (3½oz) toasted almonds,
  chopped
2 tbsp pumpkin seeds
2 tbsp sunflower seeds
100g (3½oz) ready-to-eat dried
  apricots, chopped
milk or yogurt to serve

1 Mix the oats with the almonds, seeds and apricots. Store in a sealable container: it will keep for up to one month. Serve with milk or yogurt.

 COOK'S TIP
Oats contain gluten and, strictly speaking, are not suitable for coeliacs. However, because they contain a much smaller amount than wheat, rye or barley, research shows that most people with coeliac disease can safely eat moderate amounts. The oats must be from a source where there is no risk of contamination from wheat or wheat products during processing or packing. As individual tolerance to gluten varies, if you are a coeliac, seek expert advice before eating oats.

Apple Compôte

Preparation Time 10 minutes, plus chlling • Cooking Time 5 minutes • Serves 2 • Per Serving 188 calories, 7g fat (of which 1g saturates), 29g carbohydrate, 0g salt • Vegetarian • Gluten Free • Easy

250g (9oz) cooking apples, peeled
   and chopped
juice of ½ lemon
1 tbsp golden caster sugar
ground cinnamon

TO SERVE
25g (1oz) raisins
25g (1oz) chopped almonds
1 tbsp natural yogurt

1 Put the cooking apples into a pan with the lemon juice, caster sugar and 2 tbsp cold water. Cook gently for 5 minutes or until soft. Transfer to a bowl.

2 Sprinkle a little ground cinnamon over the top, cool and chill. It will keep for up to three days.

3 Serve with the raisins, chopped almonds and yogurt.

⭐ COOK'S TIP
To microwave, put the apples, lemon juice, sugar and water into a microwave-proof bowl, cover loosely with clingfilm and cook on full power in an 850W microwave oven for 4 minutes or until the apples are just soft.

Classic French Omelette

Preparation Time 5 minutes • **Cooking Time** 5 minutes • **Serves 1** • **Per Serving** 449 calories, 40g fat (of which 19g saturates), 1g carbohydrate, 1g salt • **Vegetarian** • **Gluten Free** • **Dairy Free** • **Easy**

2–3 medium eggs
1 tbsp milk or water
25g (1oz) unsalted butter
salt and ground black pepper
sliced or grilled tomatoes and
freshly chopped flat-leafed
parsley to serve

1 Whisk the eggs in a bowl, just enough to break them down – over-beating spoils the texture of the omelette. Season with salt and pepper and add the milk or water.

2 Heat the butter in an 18cm (7in) omelette pan or non-stick frying pan until it is foaming, but not brown. Add the eggs and stir gently with a fork or wooden spatula, drawing the mixture from the sides to the centre as it sets and letting the liquid egg in the centre run to the sides. When set, stop stirring and cook for 30 seconds or until the omelette is golden brown underneath and still creamy on top: don't overcook. If you are making a filled omelette (see Try Something Different), add the filling at this point.

3 Tilt the pan away from you slightly and use a palette knife to fold over one-third of the omelette to the centre, then fold over the opposite third. Slide the omelette out on to a warmed plate, letting it flip over so that the folded sides are underneath. Serve immediately, with tomatoes sprinkled with parsley.

★ TRY SOMETHING DIFFERENT
• Blend 25g (1oz) mild goat's cheese with 1 tbsp crème fraîche; put in the centre of the omelette before folding.
• Toss 25g (1oz) chopped smoked salmon or cooked smoked haddock with a little chopped dill and 1 tbsp crème fraîche; scatter over the omelette before folding.

Creamy Baked Eggs

Preparation Time 5 minutes • Cooking Time 15–18 minutes • Serves 4 • Per Serving 153 calories, 14g fat
(of which 7g saturates), 1g carbohydrate, 0.2g salt • Vegetarian • Gluten Free • Easy

butter to grease
4 sun-dried tomatoes
4 medium eggs
4 tbsp double cream
salt and ground black pepper
Granary bread to serve (optional)

1 Preheat the oven to 180°C (160°C fan oven) mark 4. Grease four individual ramekins.

2 Put a tomato into each ramekin and season to taste with salt and pepper. Carefully break an egg on top of each tomato, then drizzle 1 tbsp cream over each egg.

3 Bake for 15–18 minutes – the eggs will continue to cook once they have been taken out of the oven.

4 Leave to stand for 2 minutes before serving. Serve with Granary bread, if you like.

Piperade

★

Preparation Time 20 minutes • Cooking Time 20 minutes • Serves 4 • Per Serving 232 calories, 17g fat (of which 4g saturates), 7g carbohydrate, 0.4g salt • Vegetarian • Gluten Free • Dairy Free • Easy

2 tbsp olive oil
1 medium onion, finely chopped
1 garlic clove, finely chopped
1 red pepper, seeded and chopped
375g (13oz) tomatoes, peeled, seeded and chopped
a pinch of cayenne pepper
8 large eggs
salt and ground black pepper
freshly chopped flat-leafed parsley to garnish
fresh bread to serve (optional)

1 Heat the oil in a heavy-based frying pan. Add the onion and cook gently for 5 minutes. Add the red pepper and cook for 10 minutes or until softened.

2 Add the tomatoes, increase the heat and cook until they are reduced to a thick pulp. Season well with cayenne pepper, salt and pepper.

3 Lightly whisk the eggs and add to the frying pan. Using a wooden spoon, stir gently until they've just begun to set but are still creamy. Garnish with parsley and serve with bread, if you like.

Poached Eggs with Mushrooms

Preparation Time 15 minutes • Cooking Time 20 minutes • Serves 4 • Per Serving 276 calories, 23g fat (of which 9g saturates), 1g carbohydrate, 0.7g salt • Vegetarian • Gluten Free • Easy

8 medium-sized flat or portabella mushrooms
40g (1½oz) butter
8 medium eggs
225g (8oz) baby spinach leaves
4 tsp fresh pesto

1 Preheat the oven to 200°C (180°C fan oven) mark 6. Arrange the mushrooms in a single layer in a small roasting tin and dot with the butter. Roast for 15 minutes or until golden brown and soft.

2 Meanwhile, bring a wide shallow pan of water to the boil. When the mushrooms are half-cooked and the water is bubbling furiously, break the eggs into the pan, spaced well apart, then take the pan off the heat. The eggs will take about 6 minutes to cook.

3 When the mushrooms are tender, put them on a warmed plate, cover and return to the turned-off oven to keep warm.

4 Put the roasting tin over a medium heat on the hob and add the spinach. Cook, stirring, for about 30 seconds or until the spinach has just started to wilt.

5 The eggs should be set by now, so divide the mushrooms among four warmed plates and top with a little spinach, a poached egg and a teaspoonful of pesto.

★ TRY SOMETHING DIFFERENT
For a more substantial meal, serve on 100% rye bread or German pumpernickel.

Scrambled Eggs with Smoked Salmon

Preparation Time 10 minutes • Cooking Time 5 minutes • Serves 4 • Per Serving 457 calories, 34g fat (of which 17g saturates), 17g carbohydrate, 2.7g salt • Easy

6 large eggs
25g (1oz) butter, plus extra to
    spread
100g (3½oz) mascarpone cheese
125g pack smoked salmon, sliced,
    or smoked salmon trimmings
6 slices sourdough or rye bread,
    toasted, buttered and cut into
    slim rectangles for soldiers
salt and ground black pepper

1 Crack the eggs into a jug and lightly beat together. Season well.

2 Melt the butter in a non-stick pan over a low heat. Add the eggs and stir constantly until the mixture thickens. Add the mascarpone and season well. Cook for 1–2 minutes longer, until the mixture just becomes firm, then fold in the smoked salmon. Serve at once with toasted bread soldiers.

Beans on Toast

Preparation Time 5 minutes • Cooking Time 10 minutes • Serves 4 • Per Serving 364 calories, 9g fat (of which 2g saturates), 55g carbohydrate, 2.1g salt • Easy

1 tbsp olive oil
2 garlic cloves, finely sliced
400g can borlotti or cannellini
    beans, drained and rinsed
400g can chickpeas
400g can chopped tomatoes
leaves from 2 fresh rosemary
    sprigs, finely chopped
4 thick slices Granary bread
25g (1oz) Parmesan
chopped fresh parsley to serve

1 Heat the oil in a pan over a low heat, add the garlic and cook for 1 minute, stirring gently.

2 Add the beans and chickpeas to the pan with the tomatoes and bring to the boil. Add the rosemary, then reduce the heat and simmer for 8–10 minutes until thickened.

3 Meanwhile, toast the bread and put on to plates. Grate the Parmesan into the bean mixture, stir once, then spoon over the bread. Serve immediately, scattered with parsley.

⭐ TRY SOMETHING DIFFERENT
This will be just as good with toasted soda bread or seeded bread, mixed beans instead of borlotti or cannellini, and grated Gruyère cheese or Cheddar instead of Parmesan.

BLT-topped Bagels with Hollandaise Sauce

Preparation Time 15 minutes • Cooking Time 8 minutes • Serves 6 • Per Serving 384 calories, 31g fat (of which 16g saturates), 16g carbohydrate, 1.9g salt • Easy

3 large bagels, cut in half horizontally
25g (1oz) butter, softened
12 smoked streaky bacon rashers, rind removed
2 tsp olive oil
3 tomatoes, cut into thick slices
150ml (¼ pint) bought hollandaise sauce (or make your own, see page 63)
75g (3oz) rocket leaves
crushed black pepper to garnish

1 Preheat the grill to high, then grill the halved bagels until golden. Spread generously with the butter. Cover the bagels with a piece of foil and keep them warm. Grill the bacon for 2–3 minutes until crisp, then keep warm. Heat the oil in a small frying pan until very hot and fry the tomatoes for about 1 minute until lightly charred.

2 Put the hollandaise sauce in a small pan and heat gently. To assemble, top the warm bagels with a few rocket leaves, the tomatoes and bacon. Spoon the warm hollandaise sauce over the bacon and garnish with the pepper. Serve at once.

Boxty Pancakes

Preparation Time 20 minutes • Cooking Time 30 minutes • Serves 6 • Per Serving 340 calories, 19g fat (of which 7g saturates), 29g carbohydrate, 2g salt • Easy

450g (1lb) floury potatoes, such as
    Maris Piper
75g (3oz) plain flour
1 tsp baking powder
150ml (¼ pint) buttermilk
4 medium eggs
2 tbsp sunflower oil
4 large rashers unsmoked bacon
15g (½oz) butter
200g (7oz) black pudding, chopped
150g (5oz) cherry tomatoes, halved
2 tbsp red wine vinegar
50ml (2fl oz) vegetable stock
2 tbsp each freshly chopped chives
    and oregano
salt and ground black pepper

1 Chop half the potatoes and put into a pan of cold water. Bring to the boil, then reduce the heat and simmer for 15–20 minutes. Mash and set aside.

2 Sift the flour, baking powder and 1½ tsp salt into a large bowl. Grate the remaining potato, then wrap in a clean teatowel and squeeze out all the moisture. Add it to the dry ingredients with the mash. Season with pepper and stir well. Mix together the buttermilk and eggs, then stir into the potato mixture.

3 Preheat the oven to 180°C (160°C fan oven) mark 4. Heat the oil in an ovenproof 23–25.5cm (9–10in) non-stick ovenproof frying pan and pour in the potato mixture. Flatten the top and turn the heat to low. Cook gently for 10 minutes or until golden underneath. Cover the pan with a plate, flip the pancake on to the plate, then slide the pancake back into the pan and cook the other side for 5 minutes. Transfer the pan to the oven and cook for 10 minutes.

4 Meanwhile, fry the bacon, slice thickly and keep warm. In the same pan, melt the butter and add the black pudding. Fry for 5 minutes, then stir in the cherry tomatoes, vinegar and stock and cook for 1 minute. Take off the heat and add most of the herbs, then season and set aside.

5 When the pancake is ready, put on to a board and slice into six. Put each slice on a plate and spoon some of the black pudding and bacon mixture over each pancake. Garnish with the remaining herbs and serve.

Breakfast Bruschetta

Preparation Time 5 minutes • Cooking Time 5 minutes • Serves 4 • Per Serving 145 calories, 1g fat (of which 0g saturates), 30g carbohydrate, 0.4g salt • Vegetarian • Easy

1 ripe banana, peeled and sliced
250g (9oz) blueberries
200g (7oz) quark cheese
4 slices pumpernickel or wheat-free
  wholegrain bread
1 tbsp runny honey

1 Put the banana into a bowl with the blueberries. Spoon in the quark cheese and mix well.

2 Toast the slices of bread on both sides, then spread with the blueberry mixture. Drizzle with the honey and serve immediately.

French Toast

Preparation Time 5 minutes • Cooking Time 10 minutes • Serves 4 • Per Finger 259 calories, 20g fat
(of which 9g saturates), 15g carbohydrate, 0.7g salt • Vegetarian • Easy

2 medium eggs
150ml (¼ pint) semi-skimmed milk
a generous pinch of freshly grated
   nutmeg or ground cinnamon
4 slices white bread, or fruit bread,
   crusts removed and each slice
   cut into four fingers
50g (2oz) butter
vegetable oil for frying
1 tbsp golden caster sugar

1 Put the eggs, milk and nutmeg or cinnamon into a shallow dish and beat together.

2 Dip the pieces of bread into the mixture, coating them well.

3 Heat half the butter with 1 tbsp oil in a heavy-based frying pan. When the butter is foaming, fry the egg-coated bread pieces in batches, until golden on both sides, adding more butter and oil as needed. Sprinkle with sugar to serve.

★ COOK'S TIPS
● *Use leftover bread for this tasty breakfast or brunch dish.*
● *For a savoury version, use white bread and omit the spice and sugar; serve with tomato ketchup, or with bacon and maple syrup.*

Orange Eggy Bread

Preparation Time 10 minutes • Cooking Time 15 minutes • Serves 4 • Per Serving 358 calories, 13g fat (of which 7g saturates), 54g carbohydrate, 1.2g salt • Vegetarian • Easy

2 large eggs
150ml (¼ pint) milk
finely grated zest of 1 orange
50g (2oz) butter
8 slices raisin bread, halved
   diagonally
1 tbsp caster sugar
vanilla ice cream and orange
   segments to serve (optional)

1 Lightly whisk the eggs, milk and orange zest together in a bowl.

2 Heat the butter in a large frying pan over a medium heat. Dip the slices of raisin bread into the egg mixture, then fry on both sides until golden.

3 Sprinkle the bread with the sugar and serve immediately with ice cream and orange slices, if you like.

Lemon and Blueberry Pancakes

⭐

Preparation Time 15 minutes • Cooking Time 10–15 minutes • Serves 4 • Per Serving 290 calories, 13g fat (of which 6g saturates), 39g carbohydrate, 0.6g salt • Vegetarian • Easy

125g (4oz) wholemeal plain flour
1 tsp baking powder
¼ tsp bicarbonate of soda
2 tbsp golden caster sugar
finely grated zest of 1 lemon
125g (4oz) natural yogurt
2 tbsp milk
2 medium eggs
40g (1½oz) butter
100g (3½oz) blueberries
1 tsp sunflower oil
natural yogurt and fruit compote
to serve

1 Sift the flour, baking powder and bicarbonate of soda into a bowl, tipping in the contents left in the sieve. Add the sugar and lemon zest. Pour in the yogurt and milk. Break the eggs into the mixture and whisk together.

2 Melt 25g (1oz) butter in a pan, add to the bowl with the blueberries and stir everything together.

3 Heat a dot of butter with the oil in a frying pan over a medium heat until hot. Add four large spoonfuls of the mixture to the pan to make four pancakes. After about 2 minutes, flip them over and cook for 1–2 minutes. Repeat with the remaining mixture, adding a dot more butter each time.

4 Serve with natural yogurt and some fruit compote.

⭐ TRY SOMETHING DIFFERENT
Instead of blueberries and lemon, use 100g (3½ oz) chopped ready-to-eat dried apricots and 2 tsp grated fresh root ginger.

Banana and Pecan Muffins

Preparation Time 10 minutes • Cooking Time 20 minutes • Makes 12 muffins • Per Muffin 236 calories, 9g fat (of which 4g saturates), 37g carbohydrate, 0.8g salt • Vegetarian • Easy

275g (10oz) self-raising flour
1 tbsp bicarbonate of soda
1 tsp salt
3 very ripe large bananas, about 450g (1lb), peeled and mashed
125g (4oz) golden caster sugar
1 large egg
50ml (2fl oz) milk
75g (3oz) melted butter
50g (2oz) chopped roasted pecan nuts

1 Preheat the oven to 180°C (160°C fan oven) mark 4. Line a muffin tin with 12 paper cases. Sift together the flour, bicarbonate of soda and salt and set aside.

2 Combine the bananas, sugar, egg and milk, then pour in the melted butter and mix well. Add to the flour mixture with the nuts, stirring quickly and gently with just a few strokes. Half-fill the muffin cases.

3 Bake for 20 minutes or until golden and risen. Transfer to a wire rack and leave to cool.

⭐ COOK'S TIP
The secret to really light, fluffy muffins is a light hand:
● *Be sure to sift the flour.*
● *Stir the mixture as little as possible; it's okay if it looks a little lumpy.*
● *Over-mixing will give tough, chewy results.*

Brazil Nut and Banana Smoothie

Preparation Time 10 minutes • Serves 2, makes 600ml (1 pint) • Per Serving 310 calories, 19g fat (of which 4g saturates), 25g carbohydrate, 0.3g salt • Vegetarian • Easy

6 shelled Brazil nuts
1 lemon
1 small ripe banana
1 small ripe avocado
1 tsp clear honey
400ml (14fl oz) low-fat dairy or
   soya milk, well chilled
2 tsp wheatgerm

1 Grind the nuts in a spice grinder or food processor – the mixture needs to be very fine to obtain a good blend.

2 Using a sharp knife, cut off the peel from the lemon, removing as much of the white pith as possible. Chop the flesh roughly, discarding any pips. Peel and roughly chop the banana. Halve the avocado and remove the stone. Peel and roughly chop.

3 Put the nuts, lemon, banana and avocado into a blender with the honey and milk. Whiz until smooth. Pour into two glasses and sprinkle with the wheatgerm.

★ COOK'S TIP
This is a lusciously thick, protein-rich drink; add more milk if you like.

Berry Uplifter

Preparation Time 5 minutes • Serves 1, makes 400ml (14fl oz) • Per Serving 277 calories, 2g fat (of which trace saturates), 62g carbohydrate, 0.1g salt • Vegetarian • Easy

175g (6oz) blueberries, thawed if frozen, juices reserved (see Cook's Tip, page 11)
50g (2oz) cranberries, thawed if frozen, juices reserved
200ml (7fl oz) freshly pressed orange juice or 2 medium oranges, juiced
1 tbsp wheatgerm
1–2 tsp thick honey

1 If using fresh berries, wash and pat them dry with kitchen paper and put into a blender. If the fruit has been frozen, add the juices as well.

2 Pour in the orange juice and add 2 tsp wheatgerm. Whiz until smooth.

3 Taste and add honey to sweeten. Pour into a glass and serve sprinkled with the remaining wheatgerm.

★ TRY SOMETHING DIFFERENT
Use blackberries instead of blueberries: they are also an excellent source of vitamin C.

Cranberry and Mango Smoothie

Preparation Time 5 minutes • Serves 2 • Per Serving 133 calories, 1g fat (of which trace saturates), 29g carbohydrate, 0.2g salt • Vegetarian • Gluten Free • Easy

1 ripe mango, peeled, stoned and
   chopped
250ml (9fl oz) cranberry juice
150g (5oz) natural yogurt

1 Put the mango into a blender with the cranberry juice and whiz for 1 minute.

2 Add the yogurt and whiz until smooth, then serve.

★ COOK'S TIP
If you're on a dairy-free diet or are looking for an alternative to milk-based products, swap the yogurt for soya yogurt. Soya is a good source of omega-3 and omega-6 essential fatty acids, and can help to lower cholesterol levels.

Green Tea Pick-me-up

Preparation Time 10 minutes, plus infusing and cooling • Serves 1, makes 300ml (½ pint) • Per Serving 99 calories, trace fat, 24g carbohydrate, 0g salt • Vegetarian • Gluten Free • Dairy Free • Easy

1 tsp, or 1 teabag, Japanese green tea
1 ripe kiwi fruit
8 fresh lychees
a few ice cubes

1 Put the tea or teabag into a heatproof jug and pour in 200ml (7fl oz) boiling water. Leave to infuse for 3 minutes, then strain to remove the tea leaves, or discard the teabag. Leave to cool.

2 When ready to serve, peel and roughly chop the kiwi fruit. Put into a blender. Peel the lychees, then cut in half and remove the stones.

3 Add to the blender with the cold tea. Whiz until smooth, then pour over ice in a glass to serve.

★ TRY SOMETHING DIFFERENT
For extra zing, add a 5cm (2in) piece fresh root ginger, peeled and chopped, to the blender in step 2.

Mango and Oat Smoothie

Preparation Time 5 minutes • Serves 2 • Per Serving 145 calories, 2g fat (of which 1g saturates), 27g carbohydrate, 0.2g salt • Vegetarian • Easy

150g (5oz) natural yogurt
1 small mango, peeled, stoned and
   chopped
2 tbsp oats
4 ice cubes

1 Put the yogurt into a blender. Set aside a little chopped mango to decorate, if you like, and add the remaining mango, oats and ice cubes to the yogurt. Whiz until smooth. Serve immediately, decorated with chopped mango.

★ TRY SOMETHING DIFFERENT
Instead of mango, use 2 nectarines or peaches, or 175g (6oz) soft seasonal fruits such as raspberries, strawberries or blueberries.

Mega Vitamin C Tonic

Preparation Time 10 minutes • Serves 1, makes 200ml (7fl oz) • Per Serving 144 calories, trace fat, 35g carbohydrate, 0g salt • Vegetarian • Gluten Free • Dairy Free • Easy

1 large orange
1 lemon
1 lime
½ pink grapefruit
1–2 tsp clear honey
crushed ice
slices of citrus fruit to decorate

1 Using a sharp knife, cut off the peel from all the citrus fruit, removing as much of the white pith as possible. Chop the flesh roughly, discarding any pips, and put into a blender.

2 Add the honey to taste and whiz for a few seconds until smooth.

3 Pour over crushed ice in a glass and decorate with citrus fruit to serve.

★ TRY SOMETHING DIFFERENT
For a refreshing, longer and less concentrated drink, divide this smoothie between two glasses and top up with sparkling mineral water.

Morning-after Detoxer

Preparation Time 10 minutes • Serves 2, makes 600ml (1 pint) • Per Serving 115 calories, 1g fat (of which trace saturates), 26g carbohydrate, 0.2g salt • Vegetarian • Gluten Free • Dairy Free • Easy

200g (7oz) cooked, peeled baby beetroot in natural juice
15g (½ oz) fresh root ginger, peeled and roughly chopped
juice of 1 lemon
150ml (¼ pint) freshly pressed carrot juice or 2 medium carrots, 250g (9oz), juiced
150ml (¼ pint) freshly pressed apple juice or 2 dessert apples, juiced

1 Roughly chop the beetroot and put into a blender with the juices from the pack.

2 Add the ginger, pour in the carrot and apple juices and whiz until smooth. Pour into two glasses and serve immediately.

★ COOK'S TIP
If you find the drink is too concentrated, thin it with a little chilled water.

★ TRY SOMETHING DIFFERENT
For a more powerful detoxer, juice 225g (8oz) raw beetroot and a 5cm (2in) piece of peeled fresh root ginger and mix with the other juices.

Brunch and Lunch

Apple, Celery, Ham and Pecan Salad

Preparation Time 10 minutes • Serves 6 • Per Serving 340 calories, 28g fat (of which 3g saturates), 10g carbohydrate, 1.6g salt • Gluten Free • Dairy Free • Easy

450g (1lb) fennel, halved
2 large Braeburn or Cox's Orange
    Pippin apples, about 450g (1lb),
    quartered, cored and sliced
75g (3oz) shelled pecan nuts
300g (11oz) cooked ham, cut into
    wide strips
1 head chicory, divided into leaves
fresh flat-leafed parsley sprigs to
    garnish

**FOR THE POPPY SEED
    DRESSING**
1 tsp clear honey
2 tsp German or Dijon mustard
3 tbsp cider vinegar
9 tbsp vegetable oil
2 tsp poppy seeds
salt and ground black pepper

1 To make the dressing, whisk together the honey, mustard, vinegar and seasoning in a small bowl. Whisk in the oil, then the poppy seeds. Set to one side.

2 Remove the central core from the fennel and slice thinly, lengthways. Place the fennel, apples, nuts, ham and chicory in a large serving bowl. Toss with the dressing and adjust the seasoning if necessary. Garnish with parsley sprigs and serve immediately.

★ TRY SOMETHING DIFFERENT
● *For a meat-free alternative, replace the ham with 150g (5oz) cubed Gruyère or Cheddar cheese.*
● ***Spicy Cumin Dressing***
Mix 2 tbsp red wine vinegar with 1 tsp ground cumin, a pinch of caster sugar and 5 tbsp olive oil. Season with salt and pepper to taste.
● ***Balsamic Dressing***
Mix 3 tbsp balsamic vinegar with 2 tbsp olive oil and 2 tsp wholegrain mustard.

Chickpea and Beetroot Salad

Preparation Time 15 minutes • Serves 4 • Per Serving 266 calories, 12g fat (of which 3g saturates), 32g carbohydrate, 0.7g salt • Gluten Free • Easy

250g (9oz) cooked and peeled
    beetroot in natural juice, roughly
    chopped
400g can chickpeas, drained and
    rinsed
50g (2oz) sultanas
20g (¾oz) fresh basil
1 medium carrot, grated
½ small white cabbage, finely
    shredded
juice of ½ lemon
150g (5oz) Greek yogurt
20g (¾oz) fresh mint, finely
    chopped
2 tbsp extra virgin olive oil
salt and ground black pepper

1 Put the beetroot and chickpeas into a large bowl. Add the sultanas, tear the basil and add, then add the carrot, cabbage and lemon juice.

2 Put the yogurt into a separate bowl. Add the mint and oil and season with salt and pepper. Spoon on to the salad and mix everything together. Serve immediately.

⭐ TRY SOMETHING
DIFFERENT
● Use parsley instead of basil, and add 4 finely chopped spring onions.
● Scatter the salad with 2 tbsp lightly toasted pumpkin seeds or sunflower seeds.

Bacon and Egg Salad

Preparation Time 10 minutes • Cooking Time 10 minutes • Serves 4 • Per Serving 360 calories, 27g fat (of which 8g saturates), 9g carbohydrate, 3.1g salt • Easy

4 medium eggs
250g (9oz) rindless smoked bacon
150g (5oz) cherry tomatoes
2 slices thick-cut sourdough bread,
    with crusts removed
2 tbsp mayonnaise
juice of ½ lemon
25g (1oz) Parmesan, freshly grated
2 Little Gem lettuces
ground black pepper

1 Heat a pan of water until simmering, add the eggs and boil for 6 minutes. Cool completely under cold water, peel and set aside.

2 Meanwhile, heat a griddle pan, then fry the bacon for 5 minutes or until crisp. Remove from the pan, chop into large pieces and leave to cool.

3 Add the tomatoes and bread to the pan and fry for 2–3 minutes until the bread is crisp and the tomatoes are starting to char. Remove from the heat, chop the bread into bite-sized croûtons and set aside.

4 To make the dressing, put the mayonnaise into a bowl and squeeze in the lemon juice. Add the Parmesan and mix, then season with pepper.

5 Separate the lettuce leaves and put into a large bowl. Add the bacon, tomatoes and croûtons, toss lightly, then divide among four plates. Cut the eggs in half and add one egg to each plate. Drizzle the dressing over the salad and serve.

Bacon, Avocado and Pinenut Salad

Preparation Time 5 minutes • Cooking Time 7 minutes • Serves 4 • Per Serving 352 calories, 34g fat (of which 6g saturates), 3g carbohydrate, 1g salt • Gluten Free • Dairy Free • Easy

125g (4oz) streaky bacon rashers, rind removed, cut into small neat pieces (lardons)
1 shallot, finely chopped
120g bag mixed baby salad leaves
1 ripe avocado
50g (2oz) pinenuts
4 tbsp olive oil
4 tbsp red wine vinegar
salt and ground black pepper

1 Put the bacon lardons into a frying pan over a medium heat for 1–2 minutes until the fat starts to run. Add the shallot and fry gently for about 5 minutes or until golden.

2 Meanwhile, divide the salad leaves among four plates. Halve, stone and peel the avocado, then slice the flesh. Arrange on the salad leaves.

3 Add the pinenuts, oil and vinegar to the frying pan and let bubble for 1 minute. Season with salt and pepper.

4 Tip the bacon, pinenuts and dressing over the salad and serve at once, while still warm.

★ TRY SOMETHING DIFFERENT
Replace the pinenuts with walnuts.

Bean and Chorizo Salad

Preparation Time 15 minutes • Serves 4 • Per Serving 295 calories, 19g fat (of which 4g saturates), 20g carbohydrate, 1.9g salt • Dairy Free • Easy

400g can borlotti beans, drained and rinsed
4 large celery sticks, finely sliced
75g (3oz) chorizo sausage, diced
2 shallots, finely chopped
2 tbsp freshly chopped flat-leafed parsley
grated zest of ½ lemon, plus 1 tbsp lemon juice
4 tbsp extra virgin olive oil
salt and ground black pepper

1 Put the borlotti beans into a large bowl and add the celery, chorizo, shallots and parsley.

2 To make the dressing, whisk together the lemon zest, lemon juice and oil in a small bowl. Season with salt and pepper and whisk again to combine.

3 Pour the dressing over the bean mixture, toss together and serve.

★ TRY SOMETHING DIFFERENT
Use mixed beans or flageolet beans instead of borlotti beans.

Chicken, Avocado and Peanut Salad

Preparation Time 15 minutes, plus chilling • Serves 4 • Per Serving 335 calories, 28g fat (of which 4g saturates), 2g carbohydrate, 0.1g salt • Gluten Free • Dairy Free • Easy

2 roast chicken breasts, about 250g (9oz) total weight, skinned and sliced
75g (3oz) watercress
2 tbsp cider vinegar
1 tsp English ready-made mustard
5 tbsp groundnut oil
1 large ripe avocado, halved, stoned, peeled and thickly sliced
50g (2oz) roasted salted peanuts, roughly chopped
salt and ground black pepper

1 Arrange the sliced chicken on top of the watercress, cover with clingfilm and chill until ready to serve.

2 Put the vinegar, mustard and oil into a bowl, season with salt and pepper and whisk together. Add the avocado and gently toss in the dressing, making sure each slice of avocado is well coated.

3 Just before serving, spoon the avocado and dressing over the chicken and watercress. Sprinkle with the chopped peanuts and serve immediately.

Spring Chicken Salad with Sweet Chilli Sauce

Preparation Time 15 minutes • Cooking Time 10 minutes • Serves 4 • Per Serving 307 calories, 15g fat (of which 3g saturates), 8g carbohydrate, 0.2g salt • Gluten Free • Dairy Free • Easy

2 tbsp groundnut oil, plus extra
   to grease
4 boneless, skinless chicken
   breasts, each cut into four strips
1 tbsp Cajun seasoning (see Cook's
   Tips)
salt and ground black pepper

FOR THE SALAD
175g (6oz) small young carrots, cut
   into thin matchsticks
125g (4oz) cucumber, halved
   lengthways, seeded and cut into
   matchsticks
6 spring onions, cut into
   matchsticks
10 radishes, sliced
50g (2oz) bean sprouts, rinsed and
   dried
50g (2oz) unsalted peanuts, roughly
   chopped
1 large red chilli, finely chopped
   (see Cook's Tips)
2 tsp sesame oil
Thai chilli dipping sauce to drizzle

1 Soak eight bamboo skewers in water for 20 minutes. Oil a baking sheet.

2 Preheat the grill. Toss the chicken strips in the Cajun seasoning, then season with salt and pepper and brush with oil. Thread on to the skewers.

3 Place the skewered chicken strips on the prepared baking sheet and cook under the hot grill for 3–4 minutes on each side until cooked through.

4 Place all the salad vegetables, peanuts and red chilli in a bowl, toss with the sesame oil and season well with salt and pepper.

5 Divide the vegetables among four plates, top with the warm chicken skewers and drizzle with the chilli sauce. Serve immediately.

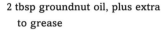 COOK'S TIPS
• *Cajun seasoning is a spice and herb mixture including chilli, cumin, cayenne and oregano.*
• *Chillies vary enormously in strength, from quite mild to blisteringly hot, depending on the type of chilli and its ripeness. Taste a small piece first to check it's not too hot for you.*
• *Be extremely careful when handling chillies not to touch or rub your eyes with your fingers, or they will sting. Wash knives immediately after handling chillies. As a precaution, use rubber gloves when preparing them, if you like.*

Easy Chicken Salad

Preparation Time 10 minutes • Serves 1 • Per Serving 323 calories, 18g fat (of which 5g saturates), 17g carbohydrate, 0.9g salt • Gluten Free • Dairy Free • Easy

100g (3½oz) shredded roast chicken, skin discarded
1 carrot, chopped
1 celery stick, chopped
¼ cucumber, chopped
a handful of ripe cherry tomatoes, chopped
1 tbsp hummus
¼ lemon to serve

1 Put the chicken into a shallow bowl. Add the carrot, celery, cucumber and cherry tomatoes.

2 Top with the hummus and serve with lemon for squeezing over the salad.

⭐ TRY SOMETHING DIFFERENT
● *For an even more nutritious salad, add a few pumpkin seeds or sunflower seeds, or a handful of sprouted seeds such as alfalfa, or chopped watercress.*
● *For extra bite, add a little finely chopped red chilli; for extra sweetness, add some strips of red pepper.*
● *For extra flavour, add some chopped coriander or torn basil leaves.*

Spring Lamb and Flageolet Bean Salad

Preparation Time 5 minutes • Cooking Time 10–20 minutes, plus resting • Serves 4 • Per Serving 535 calories, 35g fat (of which 11g saturates), 17g carbohydrate, 1.4g salt • Gluten Free • Dairy Free • Easy

2–3 lamb fillets, about 700g (1½lb) in total
1 tbsp Dijon mustard
5 tbsp olive oil
1 tsp freshly chopped parsley
2 garlic cloves
juice of 1 lemon
400g can flageolet or cannellini beans, drained and rinsed
125g (4oz) frisée lettuce or curly endive
250g (9oz) baby plum or cherry tomatoes, halved
salt and ground black pepper

1 Rub the lamb fillets with the mustard and season with pepper. Put 1 tbsp oil in a non-stick frying pan and fry the lamb over a medium heat for 5–7 minutes on each side for medium-rare, 8–10 minutes for well done. Remove the lamb, cover and set aside for 5 minutes. This allows the meat to relax, which makes slicing easier.

2 To make the dressing, put the parsley, garlic, lemon juice and remaining oil into a food processor and whiz for 10 seconds.

Alternatively, put the ingredients into a screw-topped jar, screw on the lid and shake to combine.

3 Put the beans, frisée or curly endive and the tomatoes into a bowl, combine with the dressing and season to taste with salt and pepper.

4 Slice the lamb into 1cm (½ in) pieces and place on top of the flageolet salad. Serve immediately.

 TRY SOMETHING DIFFERENT
For a vegetarian alternative, skewer the whole tomatoes on soaked wooden kebab sticks, alternating with small balls of mozzarella cheese. Grill the kebabs and drizzle with 2 tbsp pesto sauce thinned with a little olive oil.

Chilli Beef Noodle Salad

Preparation Time 15 minutes, plus soaking • Serves 4 • Per Serving 286 calories, 11g fat (of which 2g saturates), 33g carbohydrate, 0.8g salt • Gluten Free • Dairy Free • Easy

150g (5oz) dried rice noodles
juice of 1 lime
1 lemongrass stalk, outside leaves
   discarded, finely chopped
1 red chilli, seeded and chopped
   (see Cook's Tips, page 42)
2 tsp finely chopped fresh root
   ginger
2 garlic cloves, crushed
1 tbsp Thai fish sauce
3 tbsp extra virgin olive oil
50g (2oz) rocket
125g (4oz) sliced cold roast beef
125g (4oz) sunblush tomatoes,
   chopped
salt and ground black pepper

1 Put the noodles into a large bowl. Pour boiling water over them to cover, then put to one side for 15 minutes.

2 Meanwhile, in a small bowl, whisk together the lime juice, lemongrass, chilli, ginger, garlic, fish sauce and oil. Season with salt and pepper.

3 While they are still warm, drain the noodles well, put into a large bowl and toss with the dressing. Allow to cool.

4 Just before serving, toss the rocket, sliced beef and chopped tomatoes with the noodles.

★ COOK'S TIP
Sunblush tomatoes are partly dried, and more moist than sun-dried tomatoes.

Oriental Beef Salad

Preparation Time 10 minutes • Cooking Time 10 minutes • Serves 4 • Per Serving 214 calories, 9g fat (of which 3g saturates), 9g carbohydrate, 2.8g salt • Gluten Free • Dairy Free • Easy

4 tbsp tamari (wheat-free Japanese soy sauce), plus extra to serve
juice of ½ lime
2 sirloin steaks, about 175g (6oz) each
1 tbsp vegetable oil
1 mango, peeled, stoned and sliced
4 spring onions, sliced
½ Chinese lettuce, finely sliced
150g (5oz) bean sprouts
1 tbsp sesame seeds, toasted
2 tbsp freshly chopped coriander
lime wedges to serve

1 Put the tamari and lime juice into a bowl and mix well. Spoon half the dressing over the steaks and set the remainder aside.

2 Heat the oil in a frying pan, add the steaks and fry for 3 minutes on each side for medium-rare, or 3–4 minutes for well done. Set aside.

3 Put the mango, spring onions, lettuce and bean sprouts into a large bowl. Add the remaining dressing and toss gently.

4 Slice the steak into 1cm (½in) strips and serve with the salad. Sprinkle with sesame seeds and coriander and serve with a wedge of lime. Serve extra tamari sauce in a small bowl.

★ TRY SOMETHING DIFFERENT
For an alternative dressing, mix 2 tbsp tamari with 1 tbsp clear honey and 1 tbsp mirin (sweet Japanese rice wine).

Guacamole Salad

Preparation Time 15 minutes • Cooking Time 20 minutes • Serves 6 • Per Serving 317 calories, 28g fat (of which 9g saturates), 7g carbohydrate, 1.3g salt • Gluten Free • Easy

3 beef tomatoes, each sliced
    horizontally into six
½ small onion, finely sliced
1 garlic clove, crushed
1 tbsp fresh coriander leaves, plus
    extra sprigs to garnish
4 ripe avocados
juice of 1 lime
200g (7oz) feta cheese, crumbled
100g (3½oz) sunblush tomatoes in
    oil
salt and ground black pepper
lime wedges to serve

1 Divide the tomato slices among six serving plates, then scatter the onion, garlic and coriander leaves over them.

2 Cut each avocado into quarters as far as the stone. Keeping the avocado whole, start at the pointed end and peel away the skin. Separate each quarter, remove the stone, then slice the pieces lengthways. Squeeze the lime juice over the slices to stop them from browning and arrange on the plates.

3 Top with the feta cheese, sunblush tomatoes and a sprig of coriander. Finish each salad with a drizzle of oil reserved from the sunblush tomatoes and season well with salt and pepper. Serve with lime wedges.

Goat's Cheese and Walnut Salad

Preparation Time 10 minutes • Serves 6 • Per Serving 428 calories, 41g fat (of which 10g saturates), 3g carbohydrate, 0.5g salt • Vegetarian • Gluten Free • Easy

1 large radicchio, shredded
2 bunches of prepared watercress, about 125g (4oz) total weight
1 red onion, finely sliced
150g (5oz) walnut pieces
200g (7oz) goat's cheese, crumbled

FOR THE DRESSING
2 tbsp red wine vinegar
8 tbsp olive oil
a large pinch of caster sugar
salt and ground black pepper

1 Whisk all the ingredients for the dressing in a small bowl and put to one side.

2 Put the radicchio, watercress and onion into a large bowl. Pour the dressing over the salad and toss well.

3 To serve, divide the salad among six plates and sprinkle the walnuts and goat's cheese on top.

Parma Ham, Onion and Rocket Salad

Preparation Time 10 minutes • Serves 4 • Per Serving 237 calories, 18g fat (of which 6g saturates), 4g carbohydrate, 1.4g salt • Gluten Free • Easy

150g (5oz) Italian marinated onions, drained, reserving 1 tbsp of the marinade (see Cook's Tips)
4 tbsp olive oil
200g (7oz) rocket
8 slices Parma ham, about 100g (3½oz)
75g (3oz) Parmesan shavings
salt and ground black pepper

1 To make the dressing, place the reserved marinade from the onions, the oil, salt and pepper into a bowl and whisk together until combined.

2 Put the onions into a large bowl with the rocket, Parma ham and dressing. Toss together and divide among four plates. Scatter the Parmesan shavings on top and serve at once.

⭐ COOK'S TIPS
● Jars of Italian marinated onions in balsamic vinegar are available in larger supermarkets and Italian delis.
● Parmesan shavings can be bought in supermarkets. To make your own, use a vegetable peeler to pare off shavings from a block of Parmesan.

Smoked Mackerel Salad

Preparation Time 15 minutes • Serves 4 • Per Serving 656 calories, 56g fat (of which 10g saturates), 16g carbohydrate, 2.4g salt • Gluten Free • Dairy Free • Easy

250g (9oz) cooked, peeled baby
   beetroot in natural juice, diced
1 tbsp olive oil
2 tsp white wine vinegar
350g (12oz) potato salad
1–2 tbsp lemon juice
4 peppered smoked mackerel fillets,
   skinned and flaked
2 tbsp freshly chopped chives, plus
   extra to garnish
salt and ground black pepper

1 Put the beetroot into a bowl. Sprinkle with the oil and vinegar, season with salt and pepper and toss together.

2 Mix the potato salad with the lemon juice to taste. Season with salt and pepper, add the mackerel and chives and toss together.

3 Pile the mackerel mixture into four bowls. Sprinkle the beetroot over the salad and garnish with chives.

Throw-it-all-together Chicken Salad

Preparation Time 10 minutes • Serves 4 • Per Serving 215 calories, 9g fat (of which 2g saturates), 9g carbohydrate, 0.6g salt • Gluten Free • Dairy Free • Easy

4 chargrilled chicken breasts, about
   125g (4oz) each, torn into strips
2 carrots, cut into strips
½ cucumber, halved lengthways,
   seeded and cut into ribbons
a handful of fresh coriander leaves,
   roughly chopped
½ head of Chinese leaves,
   shredded
4 handfuls of watercress
4 spring onions, shredded

FOR THE DRESSING
5 tbsp peanut butter
2 tbsp sweet chilli sauce
juice of 1 lime
salt and ground black pepper

1 Put the chicken strips and all the salad ingredients into a large salad bowl.

2 To make the dressing, put the peanut butter, chilli sauce and lime juice into a small bowl and mix well. Season with salt and pepper. If the dressing is too thick to pour, add 2–3 tbsp cold water, a tablespoon at a time, to thin it – use just enough water to make the dressing the correct consistency.

3 Drizzle the dressing over the salad, toss gently together and serve.

★ COOK'S TIPS
● *Use leftover roast chicken or beef, or cooked ham.*
● *Use washed and prepared salad instead of the Chinese leaves and watercress.*

Tuna, Bean and Red Onion Salad

Preparation Time 5 minutes • Serves 4 • Per Serving 190 calories, 6g fat (of which 1g saturates), 15g carbohydrate, 1.1g salt • Gluten Free • Dairy Free • Easy

400g can cannellini beans, drained
    and rinsed
1 small red onion, very finely sliced
1 tbsp red wine vinegar
225g can tuna steak in oil (see
    Cook's Tip)
2 tbsp freshly chopped parsley
salt and ground black pepper
green salad and warm crusty bread
    to serve

1 Put the cannellini beans, onion and vinegar into a bowl, season with a little salt and mix well. Add the tuna with its oil, breaking the fish into large flakes.

2 Add half the parsley and season generously with pepper. Toss the salad, then scatter the remaining parsley over the top. Serve with a green salad and plenty of warm crusty bread.

 COOK'S TIP
Buy tuna steak canned in extra virgin olive oil, which flakes easily into large, meaty flakes and has a good flavour.

Warm Broad Bean and Feta Salad

Preparation Time 10 minutes • Cooking Time 5 minutes • Serves 2 • Per Serving 321 calories, 22g fat (of which 8g saturates), 15g carbohydrate, 1.8g salt • Vegetarian • Gluten Free • Easy

225g (8oz) broad beans – if using fresh beans you will need to start with 700g (1½lb) pods
100g (3½oz) vegetarian feta cheese, chopped
2 tbsp freshly chopped mint
2 tbsp extra virgin olive oil
a squeeze of lemon juice
salt and ground black pepper
lemon wedges to serve

1 Cook the beans in lightly salted boiling water for 3–5 minutes until tender. Drain, then plunge them briefly into cold water and drain again.

2 Tip the beans into a bowl and add the feta, mint, oil and lemon juice. Season well with salt and pepper and toss together. Serve with lemon wedges.

Warm Lentil Salad

Preparation Time 15 minutes • Cooking Time 10 minutes • Serves 2 • Per Serving 300 calories, 10g fat
(of which 2g saturates), 33g carbohydrate, trace salt • Vegetarian • Gluten Free • Dairy Free • Easy

2 medium eggs
2 tsp olive oil
2 small leeks, trimmed and
    chopped
4 spring onions, chopped
1 red pepper, seeded and chopped
400g can lentils, drained
150ml (¼ pint) vegetable stock
a handful of rocket leaves
salt and ground black pepper

1 Gently lower the eggs into a pan
of boiling water, then reduce the
heat and simmer for 7 minutes.

2 Meanwhile, heat the oil in a
separate pan and fry the leeks,
spring onions and red pepper for
6–8 minutes until softened.

3 Stir in the lentils and stock and
bring to the boil, then reduce the
heat and simmer for 1–2 minutes.
Shell the eggs, then cut in half.
Season the lentil mixture with salt
and pepper, then divide between
two bowls and top each with an egg
and a few rocket leaves.

Warm Pear and Walnut Caesar Salad

Preparation Time 10 minutes • Cooking Time 5 minutes • Serves 6 • Per Serving 397 calories, 31g fat (of which 8g fat saturates), 19g carbohydrate, 1.3g salt • Easy

50g (2oz) walnut pieces
1 tbsp walnut or mild olive oil
a small knob of butter
3 firm rosy pears, quartered, cored and thickly sliced
1 bag Caesar salad with croûtons, dressing and Parmesan
100g (3½oz) blue cheese, such as Roquefort, Stilton or Danish blue, crumbled
1 bunch of chives, roughly chopped

1 Put the walnuts into a non-stick frying pan and dry-fry over a medium heat for about 1 minute until lightly toasted. Set aside.

2 Heat the oil and butter in the frying pan, then add the pears. Fry for 2 minutes on each side or until golden. Remove with a slotted spoon.

3 To serve, put the salad leaves into a large bowl. Add the walnuts, pears, croûtons, Parmesan and blue cheese. Add the salad dressing and toss lightly, or serve the dressing separately in a small bowl. Serve immediately, garnished with chives.

★ GET AHEAD

To prepare ahead *Complete the recipe to the end of step 2, then leave the pears in the frying pan and set aside for up to 4 hours.*
To use *Warm the pears in the pan for 1 minute, then complete the recipe.*

Warm Bacon Salad

Preparation Time 10 minutes • Cooking Time 10–15 minutes • Serves 2 • Per Serving 375 calories, 29g fat
(of which 9g saturates), 11g carbohydrate, 1.7g salt • Easy

4 handfuls of soft salad leaves
1 small red onion, thinly sliced
75g (3oz) cubed pancetta
1 thick slice white bread, diced
2 medium eggs
25g (1oz) Parmesan shavings (see
   Cook's Tips, page 50)
salt and ground black pepper

FOR THE DRESSING
1 tbsp Dijon mustard
2 tbsp red wine vinegar
2 tbsp fruity olive oil

1 Put the salad leaves and onion into a large bowl. Fry the pancetta in a non-stick frying pan until it begins to release some fat. Add the diced bread and continue to fry until the pancetta is golden and crisp.

2 Put all the dressing ingredients into a small bowl, season with salt and pepper and whisk together.

3 Half-fill a small pan with cold water and bring to the boil. Turn the heat right down – there should be just a few bubbles on the base of the pan. Break the eggs into a cup,

then tip them gently into the pan and cook for 3–4 minutes, using a metal spoon to baste the tops with a little of the hot water. Lift the eggs out of the water with a slotted spoon and drain on kitchen paper.

4 Tip the pancetta, bread and any pan juices over the salad leaves. Add the Parmesan, then pour the dressing over the salad. Toss well, then divide between two plates. Top each with an egg, season to taste and serve.

Warm Spicy Chorizo and Chickpea Salad

Preparation Time 15 minutes • Cooking Time about 15 minutes • Serves 6 • Per Serving 365 calories, 24g fat (of which 6g saturates), 27g carbohydrate, 1.3g salt • Dairy Free • Easy

5 tbsp olive oil
200g (7oz) chorizo or spicy
  sausage, thinly sliced
225g (8oz) red onion, chopped
1 large red pepper, seeded and
  roughly chopped
3 garlic cloves, finely chopped
1 tsp cumin seeds
2 × 400g cans chickpeas, drained
  and rinsed
2 tbsp freshly chopped coriander
juice of 1 lemon
salt and ground black pepper

1 Heat 1 tbsp oil in a non-stick frying pan and cook the chorizo or spicy sausage over a medium heat for 1–2 minutes until lightly browned. Remove the chorizo with a slotted spoon and put to one side. Fry the onion in the chorizo oil for 8–10 minutes until browned.

2 Add the red pepper, garlic, cumin and chickpeas to the onion and cook for a further 5 minutes, stirring frequently to prevent sticking.

3 Remove the pan from the heat and add the chorizo, coriander, lemon juice and remaining oil. Season well and serve immediately.

Salmon Niçoise

Preparation Time 15 minutes • Cooking Time 6 minutes • Serves 4 • Per Serving 290 calories, 16g fat (of which 3g saturates), 16g carbohydrate, 1.7g salt • Gluten Free • Dairy Free • Easy

4 medium eggs
400g can mixed beans, drained and
　rinsed
50g (2oz) pitted black olives
250g (9oz) cherry tomatoes, halved
a large handful of mixed salad
　leaves
1 tbsp olive oil
juice of ½ lemon
200g (7oz) cooked salmon flakes
salt and ground black pepper

1 Cook the eggs in a pan of simmering water for 6 minutes. Drain the eggs, then shell and cut into quarters.

2 Put the beans into a salad bowl with the olives, tomatoes and salad leaves. Add the oil and lemon juice, season with salt and pepper and toss together. Divide among four plates, add the egg and salmon and serve.

★ TRY SOMETHING DIFFERENT
For a more traditional Niçoise salad, replace the salmon with a 300g (11oz) fresh tuna steak, cooked and flaked, and use 250g (9oz) cooked green beans instead of the mixed beans. Scatter with chopped anchovy fillets and flat-leafed parsley.

Roasted Vegetable Tartlets

Preparation Time 15 minutes • Cooking Time about 7 minutes • Makes 6 • Per Tartlet 356 calories, 24g fat (of which 1g saturates), 30g carbohydrate, 1.1g salt • Vegetarian • Easy

375g pack ready-rolled puff pastry, thawed if frozen

plain flour to dust

1 medium egg, beaten

2 tbsp coarse sea salt

300g (11oz) vegetable antipasti in olive oil

olive oil, if needed

2 tbsp balsamic vinegar

190g tub red pepper hummus

50g (2oz) wild rocket

salt and ground black pepper

1 Preheat the oven to 220°C (200°C fan oven) mark 7. Unroll the puff pastry on a lightly floured surface and cut it into six squares. Put the pastry squares on a large baking sheet and prick each one all over with a fork. Brush the surface with beaten egg and sprinkle the edges with sea salt. Bake for 5–7 minutes until the pastry is golden brown and cooked through. Press down the centre of each tartlet slightly with the back of a fish slice.

2 Make the dressing. Pour 4 tbsp oil from the jar of antipasti into a bowl (top it up with a little more olive oil if there's not enough in the antipasti jar). Add the vinegar, season with salt and pepper and mix well, then set aside.

3 To serve, spread some hummus over the central part of each tartlet. Put the tartlets on individual plates and spoon on the antipasti – there's no need to be neat. Whisk the balsamic vinegar dressing. Add the rocket leaves and toss to coat, then pile a small handful of leaves on top of each tartlet. Serve immediately.

★ GET AHEAD

To prepare ahead *Complete the recipe to the end of step 1. Leave the tartlets to cool on a wire rack, then store in an airtight container. It will keep for up to two days.*

To use *Complete the recipe.*

Egg and Pepper Pizza

Preparation Time 15 minutes • Cooking Time 12 minutes • Serves 4 • Per Serving 403 calories, 13g fat (of which 2g saturates), 61g carbohydrate, 1g salt • Vegetarian • Gluten Free • Easy

- 150g (5oz) red and yellow marinated peppers in oil, drained and oil reserved
- 8 tbsp passata
- 4 small wheat-free pizza bases
- 4 medium eggs
- 125g (4oz) watercress, washed and stalks removed

1 Preheat the oven to 220°C (200°C fan oven) mark 7. Put two large baking sheets, big enough to hold two pizzas each, into the oven to heat up.

2 Chop the peppers into thin strips. Spoon 2 tbsp passata over each pizza base and scatter strips of pepper around the edges. Make a dip in the passata in the middle of each pizza and break an egg into it. Carefully slide the pizzas on to the preheated baking sheets. Place in the oven and cook for 12 minutes or until the egg is thoroughly cooked.

3 Top the pizzas with the watercress, drizzle with a little of the reserved oil from the peppers and serve.

★ COOK'S TIP
Watercress is the salad superfood par excellence. It is a good source of iron, and vitamins C and E.

Eggs Benedict

Preparation Time 15 minutes • Cooking Time 10 minutes • Serves 4 • Per Serving 402 calories, 33g fat (of which 18g saturates), 14g carbohydrate, 1.6g salt • Easy

4 slices bread
4 medium eggs
150ml (¼ pint) Hollandaise Sauce (see Cook's Tip)
4 thin slices lean ham
parsley sprigs to garnish

1 Toast the bread on both sides. Poach the eggs. Gently warm the Hollandaise Sauce.

2 Top each slice of toast with a folded slice of ham, then with a poached egg. Finally, coat with Hollandaise Sauce.

3 Garnish each with a sprig of parsley and serve.

★ TRY SOMETHING DIFFERENT
Eggs Florentine
Cook 900g (2lb) washed spinach in a pan with a little salt until tender. Drain well, chop and reheat with 15g (½oz) butter. Melt 25g (1oz) butter, stir in 3 tbsp plain flour and cook gently for 1 minute, stirring. Remove from the heat and gradually stir in 300ml (½ pint) milk. Bring to the boil and cook, stirring, until thickened. Add 50g (2oz) grated Gruyère cheese or Cheddar and season. Do not allow to boil. Poach the eggs. Place the spinach in an ovenproof dish, arrange the eggs on top and pour the cheese sauce over them. Sprinkle with 25g (1oz) grated cheese and brown under the grill.

★ COOK'S TIP
Hollandaise Sauce
Put 4 tbsp white wine vinegar, a blade of mace, 1 slice of onion, 1 bay leaf and 6 black peppercorns into a pan. Bring to the boil and reduce to 1 tbsp liquid. Cut 150g (5oz) unsalted butter into ten pieces. Put 3 medium egg yolks into a heatproof bowl with one piece of butter and a pinch of salt. Beat, then strain in the vinegar mixture. Place over a pan of hot water, making sure the base of the bowl doesn't touch the water. Whisk for 3 minutes until pale and starting to thicken. Add a piece of butter and beat until completely absorbed. Repeat with the remaining pieces of butter. Make sure the sauce doesn't get too hot during cooking. Season and add lemon juice to taste. Serves 6.

Courgette and Parmesan Frittata

Preparation Time 10 minutes • Cooking Time 15–20 minutes • Serves 4 • Per Serving 229 calories, 19g fat (of which 9g saturates), 2g carbohydrate, 0.6g salt • Vegetarian • Gluten Free • Easy

40g (1½oz) butter
1 small onion, finely chopped
225g (8oz) courgettes, finely sliced
6 medium eggs, beaten
25g (1oz) Parmesan, freshly grated, plus shavings to garnish (see Cook's Tips, pages 50 and 204)
salt and ground black pepper
green salad to serve

1 Melt 25g (1oz) butter in an 18cm (7in) non-stick frying pan and cook the onion for about 10 minutes or until softened. Add the courgettes and fry gently for 5 minutes or until they begin to soften.

2 Beat the eggs in a bowl and season with salt and pepper.

3 Add the remaining butter to the pan and heat, then pour in the eggs. Cook for 2–3 minutes until golden underneath and cooked around the edges. Meanwhile, preheat the grill to medium.

4 Sprinkle the grated cheese over the frittata and grill for 1–2 minutes until just set. Scatter with Parmesan shavings, cut into quarters and serve with a green salad.

★ TRY SOMETHING DIFFERENT
Cherry Tomato and Rocket Frittata
Replace the courgettes with 175g (6oz) ripe cherry tomatoes, frying them for 1 minute only, until they begin to soften. Immediately after pouring in the eggs, scatter 25g (1oz) rocket leaves over the surface. Continue cooking as in step 3.

Potato and Chorizo Tortilla

Preparation Time 5 minutes • Cooking Time 25 minutes • Serves 4 • Per Serving 431 calories, 32g fat (of which 7g saturates), 23g carbohydrate, 0.9g salt • Dairy Free • Easy

6 tbsp olive oil
450g (1lb) potatoes, very thinly
 sliced
225g (8oz) onions, thinly sliced
2 garlic cloves, finely chopped
50g (2oz) chorizo sausage, cut into
 thin strips
6 large eggs, lightly beaten
salt and ground black pepper

1 Heat the oil in an 18cm (7in) non-stick frying pan over a medium-low heat. Add the potatoes, onions and garlic and stir together until coated in the oil. Cover the pan, then cook gently, stirring from time to time, for 10–15 minutes until the potato is soft. Season with salt, then add the chorizo.

2 Preheat the grill until hot. Season the beaten eggs with salt and pepper, then pour over the potato mixture. Cook over a medium heat for 5 minutes or until the edges are beginning to brown and the egg is about three-quarters set. Put the pan under the grill to brown the top. The egg should be a little soft in the middle, as it continues to cook and set as it cools. Leave to cool.

3 Using a flexible turner or spatula, carefully loosen the tortilla around the edge and underneath. Cut into wedges and serve.

Mixed Mushroom Frittata

Preparation Time 15 minutes • Cooking Time 15–20 minutes • Serves 4 • Per Serving 148 calories, 12g fat (of which 3g saturates), 0g carbohydrate, 0.3g salt • Vegetarian • Dairy Free • Gluten Free

1 tbsp olive oil
300g (11oz) mixed mushrooms, sliced
2 tbsp freshly chopped thyme
zest and juice of ½ lemon
50g (2oz) watercress, chopped
6 medium eggs, beaten
salt and ground black pepper
stoneground wholegrain bread (optional) and a crisp green salad to serve

1 Heat the oil in a large deep frying pan over a medium heat. Add the mushrooms and thyme and stir-fry for 4–5 minutes until starting to soften and brown. Stir in the lemon zest and juice, then bubble for 1 minute. Lower the heat.

2 Preheat the grill. Add the watercress to the beaten eggs, season with salt and pepper and pour into the pan. Cook on the hob for 7–8 minutes until the sides and base are firm but the centre is still a little soft.

3 Transfer to the grill and cook for 4–5 minutes until just set. Cut into wedges and serve with chunks of bread, if you like, and a salad.

Quick Crab Cakes

Preparation Time 15 minutes • Cooking Time 6 minutes • Serves 4 • Per Serving 124 calories, 4g fat
(of which 1g saturates), 12g carbohydrate, 0.9g salt • Dairy Free • Easy

200g (7oz) fresh crabmeat
2 spring onions, finely chopped
2 red chillies, seeded and finely
**   chopped (see Cook's Tips,**
**   page 42)**
finely grated zest of 1 lime
4 tbsp freshly chopped coriander
about 40g (1½oz) wholemeal
**   breadcrumbs**
1 tbsp groundnut oil
1 tbsp plain flour
salt and ground black pepper
1 red chilli, seeded and thinly
**   sliced, to garnish (see Cook's**
**   Tips, page 42)**
1 lime, cut into wedges, and salad
**   leaves to serve**

1 Put the crabmeat into a bowl, then add the spring onions, chillies, lime zest, coriander and seasoning and stir to mix. Add enough breadcrumbs to hold the mixture together, then form into four small patties.

2 Heat ½ tbsp oil in a pan. Dredge the patties with flour and fry on one side for 3 minutes. Add the rest of the oil, then turn the patties over and fry for a further 2–3 minutes. Garnish the crab cakes with the sliced red chilli and serve with lime wedges to squeeze over them, and salad leaves.

★ COOK'S TIP
Use leftover bread to make breadcrumbs and then freeze them – they're a great timesaver. You can use them from frozen.

Roasted Venison Sausages

Preparation Time 10 minutes • Cooking Time 35 minutes • Serves 6 • Per Serving 439 calories, 32g fat (of which 12g saturates), 28g carbohydrate, 2.4g salt • Dairy Free • Easy

12 venison sausages
2 tbsp redcurrant jelly
1 tsp lemon juice
mashed potatoes to serve

**FOR THE RED ONION
   MARMALADE**
400g (14oz) red onions, chopped
2 tbsp olive oil
4 tbsp red wine vinegar
2 tbsp demerara sugar
1 tsp juniper berries, crushed

1 Preheat the oven to 220°C (200°C fan oven) mark 7. Put the sausages into a small roasting tin. Mix together the redcurrant jelly and lemon juice and spoon over the sausages. Roast for 35 minutes, turning once.

2 Meanwhile, make the red onion marmalade. Gently fry the onions in the oil for 15–20 minutes. Add the vinegar, sugar and juniper berries, and continue cooking for 5 minutes or until the onions are really tender.

3 Serve the sausages with the red onion marmalade and mashed potatoes.

⭐ TRY SOMETHING DIFFERENT

Fried sausages
Melt a little fat in a frying pan, add the sausages and fry for 15–20 minutes, keeping the heat low to prevent them burning and turning them once or twice to brown them evenly.

Grilled sausages
Heat the grill to hot, put the sausages on the grill rack in the grill pan and cook until one side is lightly browned, then turn them; continue cooking and turning them frequently for 15–20 minutes, until the sausages are well browned.

Baked sausages
Heat the oven to 200°C (180°C fan oven) mark 6. Put the sausages into a greased baking tin and cook in the centre of the oven for 30 minutes.

Kilted sausages
Wrap rinded streaky bacon rashers around pairs of chipolatas and bake in the same way as above at 190°C (170°C fan oven) mark 5.

Steak Sandwich

Preparation Time 5 minutes · Cooking Time 7–10 minutes · Makes 4 · Per Serving 480 calories, 11g fat (of which 3g saturates), 67g carbohydrate, 2.1g salt · Easy

2 sirloin steaks
1 tbsp olive oil
4 large mushrooms, sliced
1 red onion, sliced
1 tbsp Dijon mustard
25g (1oz) butter
2 ciabattas, halved and split
salt and ground black pepper

1 Heat a frying pan. Rub the steaks with 1 tsp oil and season. Cook for 2 minutes per side for rare, 3 minutes for medium-rare. Remove the steaks and leave to rest for 5 minutes.

2 Reduce the heat and heat the remaining oil in the pan. Stir-fry the mushrooms and onion for 5 minutes or until tender. Stir in the mustard and butter and remove from the heat.

3 Thinly slice the steak and divide between the two ciabattas. Top with the vegetables and the top half of the bread and serve.

Bloody Mary Soup with Bruschetta

Preparation Time 15 minutes, plus marinating and chilling • Cooking Time 5 minutes • Serves 4 • Per Serving 468 calories, 23g fat (of which 4g saturates), 52g carbohydrate, 1.5g salt • Dairy Free • Easy

700g (1½lb) ripe plum tomatoes, thinly sliced
6 spring onions, trimmed and finely chopped
grated zest of ½ lemon
2 tbsp freshly chopped basil, plus fresh basil leaves to garnish
125ml (4fl oz) extra virgin olive oil, plus extra to drizzle
2 tbsp balsamic vinegar
2–3 garlic cloves, crushed
a pinch of sugar
50ml (2fl oz) chilled vodka
a few drops of Tabasco
150ml (¼ pint) tomato juice

8 thin slices bruschetta
salt and ground black pepper

1 Put the tomatoes into a large shallow dish and scatter with the spring onions, lemon zest and basil.

2 Blend together the oil, vinegar, 1 crushed garlic clove, the sugar, vodka, Worcestershire sauce and Tabasco. Season to taste with salt and pepper and pour over the tomatoes. Cover and leave to marinate for 2 hours at room temperature.

3 Put the tomato salad and tomato juice into a blender and whiz until very smooth. Transfer to a bowl and leave to chill in the fridge for 1 hour.

4 Just before serving, preheat the grill. Put the bread on the grill rack and toast lightly on both sides. Rub each one with the remaining crushed garlic, drizzle with oil and garnish with fresh basil leaves. Spoon the soup into bowls, drizzle with oil, sprinkle with black pepper and serve at once with the bruschetta.

 ★ COOK'S TIP
This recipe is not suitable for children because it contains alcohol.

Broccoli and Goat's Cheese Soup

Preparation Time 10 minutes • Cooking Time 20 minutes • Serves 6 • Per Serving 220 calories, 16g fat (of which 10g saturates), 8g carbohydrate, 0.5g salt • Easy

50g (2oz) butter
2 medium onions, chopped
1 litre (1¾ pints) vegetable, chicken or turkey stock
700g (1½lb) broccoli, broken into florets, stout stalks peeled and chopped
1 head of garlic, separated into cloves, unpeeled
1 tbsp olive oil
150g (5oz) goat's cheese
salt and ground black pepper

1 Preheat the oven to 200°C (180°C fan oven) mark 6. Melt the butter in a pan over a gentle heat. Add the onions, then cover the pan and cook for 4–5 minutes until translucent. Add half the stock and bring to the boil. Add the broccoli and return to the boil, then cover the pan, reduce the heat and simmer for 15–20 minutes until the broccoli is tender.

2 Toss the cloves of garlic in the oil and tip into a roasting tin. Roast in the oven for 15 minutes or until soft when squeezed.

3 Leave the soup to cool a little, then add the goat's cheese and whiz in batches in a blender or food processor until smooth. Return the soup to the pan and add the remaining stock. Reheat gently on the hob and season to taste with salt and pepper.

4 Ladle the soup into warmed bowls, squeeze the garlic out of their skins and scatter over the soup, add a sprinkling of black pepper and serve.

 TRY SOMETHING DIFFERENT
● *Double the quantity of goat's cheese if you prefer a stronger taste.*
● *Instead of goat's cheese, substitute a soft garlic cheese for a really garlicky flavour.*

Full-of-goodness Broth

Preparation Time 10 minutes • Cooking Time 6–8 minutes • Serves 4 • Per Serving 107 calories, 4g fat (of which trace saturates), 9g carbohydrate, 1g salt • Vegetarian • Gluten Free • Dairy Free • Easy

1–2 tbsp medium curry paste (see Cook's Tip)
200ml (7fl oz) reduced-fat coconut milk
600ml (1 pint) hot vegetable stock
200g (7oz) smoked tofu, cubed
2 pak choi, chopped
a handful of sugarsnap peas
4 spring onions, chopped
lime wedges to serve

1 Heat the curry paste in a pan for 1–2 minutes. Add the coconut milk and hot stock and bring to the boil.

2 Add the smoked tofu, pak choi, sugarsnap peas and spring onions. Reduce the heat and simmer for 1–2 minutes.

3 Ladle into warmed bowls and serve with a wedge of lime to squeeze over the broth.

★ TRY SOMETHING DIFFERENT
Replace the smoked tofu with shredded leftover roast chicken and simmer for 2–3 minutes.

★ COOK'S TIP
Check the ingredients in the curry paste: some may not be suitable for vegetarians.

Teriyaki Tuna with Noodle Broth

Preparation Time 10 minutes • Cooking Time 10 minutes • Serves 4 • Per Serving 411 calories, 11g fat (of which 3g saturates), 43g carbohydrate, 0.6g salt • Dairy Free • Easy

2 tbsp teriyaki marinade
juice of ½ lime
1 tbsp sweet chilli sauce
1 tbsp honey
4 tuna steaks, 125g (4oz) each
750ml (1¼ pints) hot vegetable
   stock
2 tbsp dry sherry
200g (7oz) medium egg noodles
200g (7oz) pak choi, roughly
   chopped
2 carrots, cut into matchsticks
250g (9oz) button mushrooms,
   sliced
freshly chopped coriander
   (optional)

1 Mix the teriyaki marinade with the lime juice, chilli sauce and honey in a large shallow dish. Add the tuna and toss to coat.

2 Put the hot stock and the sherry into a pan and bring to the boil. Add the noodles and cook for 4–5 minutes, then stir in the pak choi, carrots and mushrooms and simmer for 1 minute.

3 Meanwhile, heat a frying pan until hot. Fry the tuna in the marinade for 2 minutes on each side or until just cooked and still slightly pink inside. Cut into thick slices.

4 When the noodles are cooked, divide among four wide bowls and spoon the broth over them. Top each with the tuna and a sprinkling of coriander, if you like, and serve.

Tomato, Pepper and Orange Soup

Preparation Time 15 minutes • Cooking Time 12 minutes • Serves 4 • Per Serving 136 calories, 1g fat (of which trace saturates), 30g carbohydrate, 1.8g salt • Gluten Free • Dairy Free • Easy

leaves from 3 fresh rosemary sprigs
400g jar roasted red peppers, drained
2 tsp golden caster sugar
1 litre (1¾ pints) tomato juice
4 very ripe plum tomatoes
300ml (½ pint) hot chicken stock
450ml (¾ pint) freshly squeezed orange juice
ground black pepper
crusty bread to serve

1 Put the rosemary leaves into a food processor or blender, add the red peppers, sugar, half the tomato juice and the tomatoes and whiz until slightly chunky.

2 Sieve the mixture into a pan, then stir in the hot stock, orange juice and the remaining tomato juice. Bring to the boil, then reduce the heat and simmer gently for about 10 minutes. Season with plenty of pepper and serve with chunks of bread.

Thai Chicken Soup

Preparation Time 5 minutes • Cooking Time 17 minutes • Serves 4 • Per Serving 175 calories, 7g fat
(of which 1g saturates), 7g carbohydrate, 1.2g salt • Gluten Free • Dairy Free • Easy

1 tbsp vegetable oil
1 small onion, sliced
300g (11oz) stir-fry chicken pieces
1–2 tbsp Thai red curry paste
600ml (1 pint) hot chicken stock
400g can chopped plum tomatoes
100g (3½oz) sugarsnap peas,
  halved if large
150g (5oz) baby sweetcorn, halved
  if large
4 tbsp freshly chopped coriander
grated zest of ½ lime, plus 4 lime
  wedges to serve

1 Heat the oil in a large frying pan
or wok over a medium heat. Add
the onion and fry for 5 minutes or
until it begins to soften. Add the
chicken and cook for a further
5 minutes or until golden brown,
then add the curry paste and fry for
another minute to warm the spices
through and release the flavours.

2 Pour in the hot stock and
tomatoes, then simmer for
5 minutes. Add the sugarsnap
peas and sweetcorn and cook
for a further minute or so until the
chicken is cooked through. Divide
the soup among four warmed
bowls, sprinkle with the coriander
and lime zest, and serve with lime
wedges to squeeze over the soup.

Snacks and
Light Bites

★

Artichoke and Goat's Cheese Toasts

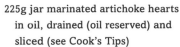

Preparation Time 15 minutes • Cooking Time 3 minutes • Serves 4 • Per Serving 371 calories, 22g fat (of which 11g saturates), 26g carbohydrate, 2.1g salt • Easy

225g jar marinated artichoke hearts in oil, drained (oil reserved) and sliced (see Cook's Tips)
225g (8oz) firm goat's cheese, rind removed, diced
1 tbsp freshly chopped thyme leaves, plus extra thyme sprigs to garnish
grated zest of 1 lemon, plus 1 tbsp lemon juice
½ tsp wholegrain mustard
4 thick slices flavoured bread, such as olive or rosemary
75g (3oz) Serrano or Parma ham slices

salt and ground black pepper
olive oil to drizzle
crushed black pepper to garnish

1 Halve the artichokes and put into a large bowl with the goat's cheese and chopped thyme.

2 Whisk together the lemon zest and juice, mustard and 3 tbsp of the reserved artichoke oil. Season with salt and pepper and whisk to combine, then stir into the artichoke mixture.

3 Toast the bread on both sides. Divide the artichoke mixture among the slices of toast and arrange the ham on top. Drizzle with a little olive oil, garnish with thyme sprigs and crushed black pepper and serve immediately.

★ COOK'S TIPS
● Find marinated artichokes in supermarkets; alternatively, buy canned artichoke hearts, drain, slice and cover in olive oil. They will keep in the fridge for up to one week.
● Serrano ham is Spanish cured ham, made in the same way as Parma ham.

Croque Monsieur

Preparation Time 5 minutes • Cooking Time 8 minutes • Serves 2 • Per Serving 551 calories, 35g fat
(of which 22g saturates), 27g carbohydrate, 3.6g salt • Easy

4 slices white bread
butter, softened, to spread, plus
   extra for frying
Dijon mustard, to taste
125g (4oz) Gruyère cheese
4 slices ham

1 Spread each slice of bread on both sides with the butter. Then spread one side of two slices of bread with a little Dijon mustard.

2 Divide the cheese and ham between the two mustard-spread bread slices. Top each with the remaining bread and press down.

3 Heat a griddle with a little butter until hot and fry the sandwiches for 2–3 minutes on each side until golden and crispy and the cheese starts to melt. Slice in half and serve immediately.

Bruschetta with Tapenade

Preparation Time 10 minutes • Cooking Time 5 minutes • Makes 12 • Per Slice 119 calories, 4g fat (of which trace saturates), 19g carbohydrate, 0.7g salt • Dairy Free • Easy

1 ciabatta loaf
olive oil to brush
6 tbsp tapenade (see Cook's Tips)
selection of vegetable antipasti,
    such as marinated red peppers
    and artichokes, drained
a few basil sprigs to garnish

1 Cut the ciabatta on the diagonal to make 12 slices. Brush both sides of the slices with a little oil. Heat a griddle pan until hot, add the ciabatta slices and toast for a couple of minutes on each side.

2 Spread a thin layer of tapenade on each slice of bread, then top with a little of the antipasti. Garnish with basil and serve. Alternatively, arrange the antipasti in separate bowls and let your guests assemble their own bruschettas.

★ COOK'S TIPS
● *Tapenade is a black olive paste from Provence in the south of France. You can buy ready-made tapenade, or make your own by whizzing 75g (3oz) pitted black olives in a food processor with 4 anchovies, 2 tbsp olive oil and 1 tbsp freshly chopped flat-leafed parsley.*
● *Instead of spreading it on bread, serve tapenade as a dip for crisp raw carrots, red pepper strips or chicory leaves.*

Grilled Ciabatta and Mozzarella Salad

Preparation Time 10 minutes • Cooking Time 5 minutes • Serves 4 • Per Serving 613 calories, 33g fat (of which 13g saturates), 56g carbohydrate, 2.4g salt • Vegetarian • Easy

8 thick slices Italian bread, such as ciabatta
2 tsp olive paste or sun-dried tomato paste
2 × 150g packs mozzarella cheese, drained and sliced (see Cook's Tips, page 204)
4 tbsp olive oil, plus extra to drizzle
2 tbsp balsamic vinegar
280g jar marinated artichoke hearts in oil, drained and sliced (see Cook's Tips, page 78)
100g (3½oz) rocket salad
50g (2oz) sun-dried tomato halves
salt and ground black pepper

1 Preheat the grill. Toast the bread slices on one side. Spread the untoasted side with olive or sun-dried tomato paste, then top with mozzarella slices and drizzle lightly with oil.

2 Mix the vinegar, salt and pepper in a bowl and whisk in the 4 tbsp oil. Add the artichoke hearts.

3 Place the bread slices under the grill for 2–3 minutes until the mozzarella browns lightly.

4 Toss the rocket salad with the artichoke mixture and divide among four plates. Top with two slices of grilled bread and the sun-dried tomatoes and serve.

Veggie Pitta

Preparation Time 8 minutes • Serves 1 • Per Serving 322 calories, 11g fat (of which 2g saturates), 47g carbohydrate, 1.2g salt • Vegetarian • Easy

1 wholemeal pitta bread
1 tbsp hummus (to make your own, see page 86), plus extra to serve
15g (½oz) unsalted cashew nuts
2 closed-cup mushrooms, finely sliced
¼ cucumber, chopped
fresh watercress or mixed salad leaves
ground black pepper

1 Split the pitta bread and spread with the hummus.

2 Fill the pitta with the cashew nuts, mushrooms, cucumber and a generous helping of fresh watercress or salad leaves. Serve with extra hummus, if you like, and season with pepper.

⭐ TRY SOMETHING DIFFERENT
Add a diced ripe avocado. It is rich in omega fats and good for your skin.

Tomato Crostini with Feta and Basil

Preparation Time 20 minutes • Cooking Time 3 minutes • Serves 4 • Per Serving 242 calories, 17g fat (of which 3g saturates), 18g carbohydrate, 1.5g salt • Vegetarian • Easy

1 small garlic clove, crushed
3 tbsp freshly chopped basil, plus
    extra basil leaves to garnish
25g (1oz) pinenuts
2 tbsp extra virgin olive oil
grated zest and juice of 1 lime
50g (2oz) vegetarian feta cheese
4 large tomatoes, preferably vine-
    ripened, thickly sliced
150g tub fresh tomato salsa
50g (2oz) pitted black olives,
    roughly chopped
4 thick slices country-style bread
salt and ground black pepper

1 Put the garlic, chopped basil, pinenuts, oil, lime zest and juice into a food processor and whiz to a smooth paste. Add the feta cheese and whiz until smooth. Thin with 1 tbsp water if necessary. Season with salt and pepper.

2 Put the tomatoes, salsa and olives into a bowl and gently toss together.

3 Toast the bread. Divide the tomato mixture among the slices of toast and spoon the basil and feta mixture on top. Garnish with basil leaves and serve.

Chicken and Salsa Verde Crostini

Preparation Time 20 minutes, plus chilling • Cooking Time 2 minutes • Makes 15 • Per Serving 208 calories, 9g fat (of which 1g saturates), 24g carbohydrate, 1.7g salt • Dairy Free • Easy

50g (2oz) walnuts
1 loaf walnut bread, cut into
    15 × 1cm (½in) slices
2 tbsp olive oil
1 tbsp sea salt flakes
175g (6oz) cooked chicken breast,
    thinly sliced
125g (4oz) sun-dried tomatoes in
    oil, drained and thinly sliced
freshly chopped flat-leafed parsley
    to garnish

FOR THE SALSA VERDE
3 tbsp each roughly chopped fresh
    coriander, mint and basil
1 garlic clove, roughly chopped
2 tbsp Dijon mustard
3 anchovy fillets
1 tbsp capers
50ml (2fl oz) olive oil
juice of ½ lemon

1 Put the walnuts into a dry pan and toast over a medium-high heat, tossing regularly, for 2–3 minutes until golden brown. Chop finely and set aside.

2 Put all the salsa verde ingredients into a food processor or blender and whiz until smooth. (Alternatively, use a pestle and mortar.) Cover and chill.

3 Preheat the grill to high. Put the bread on a baking sheet, brush with oil and sprinkle with sea salt flakes. Grill for 1 minute on each side or until lightly toasted.

4 To serve, put two or three chicken slices on each crostini base, top with a spoonful of salsa verde and slices of sun-dried tomato, then garnish with a sprinkling of walnuts and flat-leafed parsley.

Easy Wrap

Preparation Time 10 minutes • Serves 4 • Per Serving 269 calories, 16g fat (of which 3g saturates), 17g carbohydrate, 1.7g salt • Easy

1 tsp salt

1 tsp ground black pepper

2 cooked chicken breasts, about 125g (4oz) each, cut into bite-size pieces

1 carrot, grated

1 avocado, halved, stoned, peeled and chopped

a small handful of rocket

juice of ½ lemon

3 tbsp mayonnaise

4 flour tortillas

1 Mix the salt with the pepper in a large bowl. Add the chicken, carrot, avocado and rocket and mix well.

2 In a separate bowl, mix the lemon juice with the mayonnaise, then spread over the tortillas. Divide the chicken mixture among the tortillas, then roll up and serve in napkins, if you like.

Hummus with Rocket and Mint

Preparation Time 15 minutes, plus chilling • Serves 6 • Per Serving 399 calories, 30g fat (of which 5g saturates), 25g carbohydrate, 0.6g salt • Vegetarian • Dairy Free • Easy

3 tbsp sherry vinegar
75ml (2½fl oz) extra virgin olive oil
150g (5oz) wild rocket
12 small fresh mint leaves
12 Peppadew peppers (mild) (see Cook's Tips)
6 tbsp sliced jalapeño chillies (see Cook's Tips)
sesame seed flatbreads and lemon wedges to serve

FOR THE HUMMUS
400g can chickpeas, drained and rinsed
juice of 1 lemon
4 tbsp tahini (see Cook's Tips)
1 garlic clove, crushed
75ml (2½fl oz) extra virgin olive oil
salt and ground black pepper

1 To make the hummus, put the chickpeas, lemon juice, tahini, garlic and oil into a food processor. Season well with salt and pepper, then whiz to a paste. Spoon the hummus into a non-metallic bowl, then cover and chill overnight.

2 To make the salad dressing, mix the vinegar with a pinch of salt in a small bowl, then add the oil and whisk to combine. Chill overnight.

3 To serve, divide the hummus among six 150ml (¼ pint) pots. Put on to six plates. Put the rocket and mint leaves into a bowl, then drizzle the dressing over them. Divide the salad, peppers, jalapeño chillies and flatbreads among the six plates. Serve with lemon wedges.

★ COOK'S TIPS
● 'Peppadew' is the brand name of preserved sweet and spicy red peppers from South Africa; they are available as mild or hot, and are sold in jars.
● Jalapeño chillies are from Mexico; they range from hot to fiery hot and when ripe they can be dark green or red; they are usually sold in jars.
● Tahini is a paste made from finely ground sesame seeds. It is sold in jars.

Pork Pittas with Salsa

Preparation Time 10 minutes • Cooking Time 10 minutes • Serves 4 • Per Serving 518 calories, 17g fat (of which 5g saturates), 58g carbohydrate, 1.3g salt • Easy

1 tbsp olive oil
500g (1lb 2oz) diced pork
4 tbsp spicy seasoning such as
   fajita seasoning
4 large pittas
100g (3½oz) Greek yogurt

FOR THE SALSA
1 ripe avocado
1 red onion, chopped
4 large tomatoes, roughly chopped
a small handful of roughly chopped
   fresh coriander
juice of 1 lime
salt and ground black pepper

1 Heat the oil in a pan over a medium heat and cook the pork, stirring, for 3–4 minutes. Add the spicy seasoning and stir to coat the pork, then cook for a further 4–5 minutes until cooked through.

2 Meanwhile, make the salsa. Halve, stone and peel the avocado, then chop. Put the onion into a bowl and add the avocado, tomatoes, coriander and lime juice. Mix well, season with salt and pepper and put to one side.

3 Toast the pittas until lightly golden, then slit down the side and stuff with the pork, a spoonful of salsa and a dollop of Greek yogurt. Serve immediately.

 COOK'S TIP
Make your own spicy seasoning by mixing 1 crushed garlic clove, 1 tsp ground ginger and ½–1 tsp cayenne pepper. Toss with the pork and complete the recipe.

Roast Mushrooms with Pesto

Preparation Time 5 minutes • Cooking Time 15 minutes • Serves 4 • Per Serving 258 calories, 23g fat (of which 6g saturates), 1g carbohydrate, 0.5g salt • Easy

8 portabella mushrooms
8 tbsp fresh Pesto (see Cook's Tip)
toasted ciabatta, salad and basil
  leaves to serve

1 Preheat the oven to 200°C (180°C fan oven) mark 6. Put the mushrooms into an ovenproof dish, then spoon 1 tbsp fresh pesto on top of each one.

2 Pour 150ml (¼ pint) boiling water into the dish, then cook for 15 minutes or until the mushrooms are soft and the topping is hot. Serve with toasted ciabatta and salad, and scatter a few small basil leaves over the mushrooms.

★ COOK'S TIP
Pesto
Put a 20g pack of roughly chopped basil into a food processor. Add 25g (1oz) finely grated Parmesan, 50g (2oz) pinenuts and 4 tbsp extra virgin olive oil and whiz to a rough paste. Alternatively, grind in a pestle and mortar. Season with salt and plenty of ground black pepper.

Mozzarella Mushrooms

Preparation Time 2–3 minutes • Cooking Time 15–20 minutes • Serves 4 • Per Serving 137 calories, 9g fat (of which 5g saturates), 5g carbohydrate, 0.4g salt • Vegetarian • Easy

8 large portabella mushrooms
8 slices marinated red pepper
8 fresh basil leaves
150g (5oz) mozzarella cheese, cut into eight slices (see Cook's Tips, page 204)
4 English muffins, halved
salt and ground black pepper
green salad to serve

1 Preheat the oven to 200°C (180°C fan oven) mark 6. Lay the mushrooms side by side in a roasting tin and season with salt and pepper. Top each mushroom with a slice of red pepper and a basil leaf. Lay a slice of mozzarella on top of each mushroom and season again. Roast in the oven for 15–20 minutes until the mushrooms are tender and the cheese has melted.

2 Meanwhile, toast the muffin halves until golden. Put a mozzarella mushroom on top of each muffin half. Serve immediately with a green salad.

Cheesy Tuna Melt

Preparation Time 5 minutes • **Cooking Time** 5 minutes • **Serves 1** • **Per Serving** 747 calories, 36g fat (of which 18g saturates), 51g carbohydrate, 3.4g salt • **Easy**

2 slices cholla bread
100g can tuna in sunflower oil, drained
75g (3oz) Gruyère cheese, sliced
1 tomato, sliced
salt and ground black pepper

1 Preheat the grill to high. Put the bread on a baking sheet and toast one side.

2 Turn the bread so that it is untoasted side up, then divide the tuna between the two pieces and top with the cheese and tomato.

3 Grill until the cheese is bubbling and golden. Season with salt and pepper and serve immediately.

★ COOK'S TIP
You can use any type of bread for this recipe.

Tuna on Toasted Olive Bread

Preparation Time 10 minutes • Cooking Time 3 minutes • Serves 4 • Per Serving 423 calories, 18g fat (of which 6g saturates), 36g carbohydrate, 2.3g salt • Easy

2 × 185g cans tuna chunks in oil, drained and oil reserved

8 spring onions, chopped

1 yellow pepper, seeded and sliced

20 kalamata olives, pitted and halved

2 tbsp extra virgin olive oil

1 tbsp white wine vinegar

1 tsp soured cream, plus extra to serve

8 thick slices olive bread

a handful of rocket

salt and ground black pepper

1 Put the tuna into a bowl with the spring onions, yellow pepper and olives.

2 In a separate bowl, whisk 2 tbsp of the reserved tuna oil with the olive oil, vinegar and soured cream. Add to the tuna mixture and toss.

3 Toast the bread until golden. Divide the tuna mixture among the slices of toast, then scatter on a handful of rocket. Serve immediately, with extra soured cream in a small bowl.

★ COOK'S TIP
If you want to cut down on the fat, omit the olive oil and replace the soured cream with fat-free Greek yogurt.

Sardines on Toast

Preparation Time 5 minutes • Cooking Time 8–10 minutes • Serves 4 • Per Serving 240 calories, 9g fat (of which 2g saturates), 25g carbohydrate, 1.6g salt • Dairy Free • Easy

4 thick slices wholemeal bread
2 large tomatoes, sliced
2 × 120g cans sardines in olive oil, drained
juice of ½ lemon
a small handful of parsley, chopped

1 Preheat the grill. Toast the slices of bread on both sides.

2 Divide the tomato slices and the sardines among the toast slices, squeeze the lemon juice over them, then put back under the grill for 2–3 minutes to heat through. Scatter the parsley over the sardines and serve immediately.

★ TRY SOMETHING DIFFERENT
Instead of sardines, use a 200g can salmon in oil.

★ COOK'S TIP
Oily fish such as sardines are one of the best sources of essential heart-protecting omega-3 oils. Eat them at least once a week. Fresh Cornish sardines, when they are available, are a treat and are cheap. Look out for them at your fishmonger's or on the fresh fish counter at the supermarket.

Prawn Poppadoms

Preparation Time 10 minutes • Cooking Time 3 minutes • Makes 24 • Per Serving 57 calories, 3g fat (of which 1g saturates), 4g carbohydrate, 0.2g salt • Gluten Free • Easy

½ tbsp sesame oil

24 raw tiger prawns, peeled and deveined (see Cook's Tip, right)

4 tbsp Sweet Chilli Sauce (see Cook's Tip, below)

150ml (¼ pint) soured cream

24 mini poppadoms

1 lime, cut into thin wedges, to serve

1 Heat the oil in a pan, then quickly fry the prawns with 2 tbsp sweet chilli sauce for 3–4 minutes until just pink.

2 Mix the remaining sweet chilli sauce with the soured cream, then spoon on to the poppadoms. Top each with a prawn and a sliver of fresh lime (assemble just before serving, otherwise the poppadoms will go soft).

★ COOK'S TIP

To devein prawns, pull off the head and discard (or put to one side and use later for making stock). Using pointed scissors, cut through the soft shell on the belly side. Prise off the shell, leaving the tail attached. (The shell can also be used later for making stock.) Using a small sharp knife, make a shallow cut along the back of the prawn. Using the point of the knife, remove and discard the black vein (the intestinal tract) that runs along the back of the prawn.

★ COOK'S TIP

Sweet Chilli Sauce

Heat 1 tbsp olive oil in a pan. Add 2 finely chopped large garlic cloves and 2 tsp tomato purée and cook for 30 seconds. Add 550g (1¼lb) tomatoes, cut into chunks, 4 large red chillies, seeded and finely chopped (see Cook's Tips, page 42), 200g (7oz) dark muscovado sugar and 100ml (3½fl oz) white wine vinegar. Bring to the boil and bubble for 30–35 minutes until reduced and pulpy. Pour the tomato mixture into a sieve and, using the back of a ladle, push through as much of the pulp as possible. Return to the pan and simmer for 5 minutes. Add salt to taste. Serves 6.

Squid with Haricot Beans and Rocket

Preparation Time 20 minutes, plus marinating • Cooking Time about 2 minutes • Serves 6 • Per Serving 317 calories, 12g fat (of which 2g saturates), 33g carbohydrate, 1.7g salt • Easy

450g (1lb) prepared squid, cut into thick rings
3 tbsp extra virgin olive oil
1 rosemary sprig, cut into four pieces
1 chilli, seeded and finely chopped (see Cook's Tips, page 42)
zest and juice of 1 lemon
2 × 400g cans haricot beans, drained and rinsed
2 tbsp olive oil
6 slices sourdough bread
55g pack rocket
salt and ground black pepper
lemon wedges to serve

1 Put the squid into a non-metallic bowl. Add 1 tbsp extra virgin olive oil, the rosemary, chilli and half the lemon zest. Season to taste with salt and pepper, then marinate for 30 minutes.

2 Put the beans into a large bowl with the remaining lemon zest and extra virgin olive oil and the lemon juice. Season with salt and pepper, then use a potato masher to pound into a rough purée.

3 Heat the olive oil in a wok or a non-stick frying pan and cook the squid for 1–2 minutes until opaque. Toast the bread.

4 Spread the bean purée over the toast. Top with the squid and rocket and serve with lemon wedges.

Smoked Haddock Rarebit

Preparation Time 5 minutes • Cooking Time 10–15 minutes • Serves 4 • Per Serving 481 calories, 32g fat
(of which 21g saturates), 16g carbohydrate, 3.4g salt • Easy

**4 × 150g (5oz) smoked haddock
fillets, skinned**
4 slices bread
200g (7oz) spinach
2 large tomatoes, sliced
300g (11oz) low-fat crème fraîche
salt and ground black pepper

1 Preheat the grill. Season the haddock fillets with salt and pepper and put into a shallow ovenproof dish. Grill for 6–8 minutes until opaque and cooked through.

2 Toast the bread on both sides until golden.

3 Wash the spinach, squeeze out the water and put into a pan. Cover and cook for 1–2 minutes until starting to wilt. Tip into a bowl.

4 Top each piece of toast with a piece of fish, then add the tomato slices and spinach. Spoon the crème fraîche over it and grill for 2–3 minutes to heat through. Season with pepper and serve immediately.

Simple Suppers

Fast Macaroni Cheese

Preparation Time 5 minutes • Cooking Time 15 minutes • Serves 4 • Per Serving 1137 calories, 69g fat (of which 44g saturates), 96g carbohydrate, 2g salt • Easy

500g (1lb 2oz) macaroni
500ml (18fl oz) crème fraîche
200g (7oz) freshly grated Parmesan
2 tbsp ready-made English or Dijon
   mustard
5 tbsp freshly chopped flat-leafed
   parsley
ground black pepper
green salad to serve

1 Cook the macaroni in a large pan of lightly salted boiling water according to the pack instructions. Drain and keep to one side.

2 Preheat the grill to high. Put the crème fraîche into a pan and heat gently. Stir in 175g (6oz) Parmesan, the mustard and parsley and season well with black pepper. Stir the pasta into the sauce, spoon into bowls and sprinkle with the remaining cheese. Grill until golden and serve immediately with salad.

Ham and Mushroom Pasta

Preparation Time 5 minutes • Cooking Time 15 minutes • Serves 4 • Per Serving 415 calories, 10g fat (of which 4g saturates), 67g carbohydrate, 1g salt • Easy

350g (12oz) penne pasta
1 tbsp olive oil
2 shallots, sliced
200g (7oz) small button mushrooms
3 tbsp crème fraîche
125g (4oz) smoked ham, roughly chopped
2 tbsp freshly chopped flat-leafed parsley
salt and ground black pepper

1 Cook the pasta in a large pan of lightly salted boiling water according to the pack instructions until al dente.

2 Meanwhile, heat the oil in a pan. Add the shallots and fry gently for 3 minutes or until starting to soften. Add the mushrooms and fry for 5–6 minutes.

3 Drain the pasta, put back into the pan and add the shallots and mushrooms. Stir in the crème fraîche, ham and parsley. Toss everything together, season to taste with salt and pepper and heat through to serve.

Pasta with Pesto and Beans

Preparation Time 5 minutes • Cooking Time 15 minutes • Serves 4 • Per Serving 738 calories, 38g fat (of which 10g saturates), 74g carbohydrate, 1g salt • Easy

350g (12oz) pasta shapes
175g (6oz) fine green beans, roughly chopped
175g (6oz) small salad potatoes, such as Anya, thickly sliced
250g (9oz) fresh Pesto sauce (see Cook's Tip, page 88)
Parmesan shavings to serve (see Cook's Tips, page 50)

1 Cook the pasta in a large pan of lightly salted boiling water according to the pack instructions for 5 minutes.

2 Add the beans and potatoes to the pan and continue to boil for a further 7–8 minutes until the potatoes are just tender.

3 Drain the pasta, beans and potatoes in a colander, then tip everything back into the pan and stir in the pesto sauce. Serve scattered with Parmesan shavings.

 COOK'S TIP
Use leftover cooked pasta, beans or potatoes: tip the pasta into a pan of boiling water and bring back to the boil for 30 seconds. Bring the beans or potatoes to room temperature, but there's no need to re-boil them.

Quick and Easy Carbonara

Preparation Time 5 minutes • Cooking Time 10 minutes • Serves 4 • Per Serving 688 calories, 39g fat (of which 19g saturates), 65g carbohydrate, 1.6g salt • Easy

350g (12oz) tagliatelle
150g (5oz) smoked bacon, chopped
1 tbsp olive oil
2 large egg yolks
150ml (¼ pint) double cream
50g (2oz) freshly grated Parmesan
2 tbsp freshly chopped parsley

1 Cook the pasta in a large pan of lightly salted boiling water according to the pack instructions. Drain.

2 Meanwhile, fry the bacon in the oil for 4–5 minutes. Add to the drained pasta and keep hot.

3 Put the egg yolks into a bowl, add the cream and whisk together. Add to the pasta with the Parmesan and parsley, toss well and serve.

Creamy Parma Ham and Artichoke Tagliatelle

Preparation Time 5 minutes • Cooking Time 12 minutes • Serves 4 • Per Serving 972 calories, 56g fat (of which 36g saturates), 97g carbohydrate, 1.1g salt • Easy

500g (1lb 2oz) tagliatelle
500ml (18fl oz) crème fraîche
280g jar roasted artichoke hearts, drained and each cut in half
80g pack Parma ham (6 slices), torn into strips
2 tbsp freshly chopped sage leaves, plus extra to garnish
salt and ground black pepper
40g (1½oz) Parmesan shavings to serve (see Cook's Tips, page 50)

1 Cook the pasta in a large pan of lightly salted boiling water according to the pack instructions.

2 Drain the pasta well, leaving a ladleful of the cooking water in the pan, then put the pasta back into the pan.

3 Add the crème fraîche to the pan with the artichoke hearts, Parma ham and sage, then stir everything together. Season well.

4 Spoon the pasta into warmed bowls, sprinkle with the Parmesan shavings and garnish with sage. Serve immediately.

Pasta with Kale, Anchovy and Crispy Bread

Preparation Time 5 minutes • Cooking Time 15 minutes • Serves 4 • Per Serving 481 calories, 14g fat (of which 2g saturates), 72g carbohydrate, 3g salt • Easy

75g (3oz) fresh breadcrumbs
300g (11oz) orecchiette or other shaped pasta
150g (5oz) kale, shredded
2 tbsp olive oil
1 red chilli, seeded and finely chopped (see Cook's Tip, page 42)
100g jar anchovies, drained and chopped
25g (1oz) freshly grated Parmesan

1 Preheat the grill to medium and toast the breadcrumbs.

2 Cook the pasta in a large pan of lightly salted boiling water according to the pack instructions until al dente. Add the kale for the last 5–6 minutes of cooking time.

3 Heat 1 tbsp oil in a pan and fry the chilli and anchovies for 3–4 minutes.

4 Drain the pasta and kale, then tip back into the pan. Add the breadcrumbs, the anchovy mixture, the remaining oil and the Parmesan. Toss to mix, then serve.

Chicken, Bacon and Leek Pasta Bake

Preparation Time 10 minutes • Cooking Time about 20 minutes • Serves 4 • Per Serving 650 calories, 24g fat (of which 6g saturates), 68g carbohydrate, 2.2g salt • Easy

1 tbsp olive oil

100g (3½oz) bacon lardons

450g (1lb) boneless, skinless chicken thighs, chopped

3 medium leeks, trimmed and chopped

300g (11oz) macaroni or other pasta shapes

350g carton ready-made cheese sauce

2 tsp Dijon mustard

2 tbsp freshly chopped flat-leafed parsley

25g (1oz) freshly grated Parmesan

1 Heat the oil in a large frying pan. Add the bacon and chicken and cook for 7–8 minutes. Add the leeks and continue cooking for 4–5 minutes.

2 Meanwhile, cook the pasta in a large pan of lightly salted boiling water according to the pack instructions. Drain well.

3 Preheat the grill. Add the cheese sauce to the pasta with the mustard, chicken mixture and parsley. Mix well, then tip into a 2.1 litre (3¾ pint) ovenproof dish and sprinkle with Parmesan. Grill for 4–5 minutes until golden.

Grilled Chicken with Mango Salsa

Preparation Time 10 minutes • Cooking Time 20 minutes • Serves 4 • Per Serving 288 calories, 14g fat (of which 4g saturates), 7g carbohydrate, 0.2g salt • Gluten Free • Dairy Free • Easy

4 chicken breasts
juice of ½ lime
oil-water spray (see Cook's Tip)
salt and ground black pepper
rocket leaves to serve

FOR THE SALSA
1 mango, peeled, stoned and diced
1 small fennel bulb, trimmed and diced
1 fresh chilli, seeded and finely diced (see Cook's Tips, page 42)
1 tbsp balsamic vinegar
juice of ½ lime
2 tbsp freshly chopped flat-leafed parsley
2 tbsp freshly chopped mint

1 Put the chicken on a grill pan and season generously with salt and pepper. Sprinkle with the lime juice and spray with the oil-water blend. Grill for 8–10 minutes on each side until cooked through and the juices run clear when pierced with a skewer. Set aside.

2 Combine all the salsa ingredients in a bowl and season generously with salt and pepper. Spoon alongside the chicken and serve with rocket leaves.

★ COOK'S TIP

Oil-water spray is far lower in calories than oil alone and, as it sprays on thinly and evenly, you'll use less. Fill one-eighth of a travel-sized spray bottle with oil such as sunflower, light olive or vegetable (rapeseed), then top up with water. To use, shake well before spraying. Store in the fridge.

Chicken Rarebit

Preparation Time 5 minutes • Cooking Time 25 minutes • Serves 4 • Per Serving 446 calories, 24g fat (of which 14g saturates), 9g carbohydrate, 1.3g salt • Easy

4 large chicken breasts, with skin, about 150g (5oz) each
15g (½oz) butter
1 tbsp plain flour
75ml (2½fl oz) full-fat milk
175g (6oz) Gruyère cheese, grated
25g (1oz) fresh white breadcrumbs
1 tsp ready-made English mustard
2 fat garlic cloves, crushed
1 medium egg yolk
boiled new potatoes and green beans to serve

1 Preheat the oven to 200°C (180°C fan oven) mark 6. Put the chicken in a single layer into an ovenproof dish and roast for 20 minutes or until cooked through.

2 Meanwhile, melt the butter in a pan over a low heat, then add the flour and stir for 1 minute. Gradually add the milk and stir to make a smooth sauce.

3 Add the cheese, breadcrumbs, mustard and garlic to the sauce and cook for 1 minute. Cool briefly, then beat in the egg yolk. Preheat the grill to medium-high.

4 Discard the skin from the cooked chicken and beat any juices from the dish into the cheese mixture. Spread the paste evenly over each chicken breast, then grill for 2–3 minutes until golden. Serve with boiled new potatoes and green beans.

Peas and Bacon with Pan-fried Chicken

Preparation Time 5 minutes • Cooking Time 20 minutes • Serves 4 • Per Serving 314 calories, 21g fat (of which 5g saturates), 7g carbohydrate, 0.9g salt • Gluten Free • Easy

4 skinless chicken breasts, about
   125g (4oz) each
2 tbsp olive oil
2 shallots, finely sliced
3 unsmoked, rindless streaky bacon
   rashers, chopped
200g (7oz) frozen peas, thawed
2 tbsp sunblush tomato pesto
salt and ground black pepper
buttered new potatoes to serve

1 Heat a griddle. Season the chicken generously with salt and pepper, then brush with 1 tbsp oil and cook on the griddle, skin side down, for 8–10 minutes. Turn over and continue to cook on the other side for 8–10 minutes until cooked through and the juices run clear when the chicken is pierced with a sharp knife.

2 Meanwhile, heat the remaining oil in a frying pan and fry the shallots and bacon until the shallots are softened and the bacon is golden. Add the peas and cook for 2 minutes, then stir in the pesto.

3 Serve the peas and bacon with the chicken breasts and new potatoes.

One-pan Chicken with Tomatoes

Preparation Time 5 minutes • Cooking Time 20–25 minutes • Serves 4 • Per Serving 238 calories, 4g fat (of which 1g saturates), 20g carbohydrate, 1g salt • Gluten Free • Dairy Free • Easy

4 chicken thighs
1 red onion, sliced
400g can chopped tomatoes with herbs
400g can mixed beans, drained and rinsed
2 tsp balsamic vinegar
freshly chopped flat-leafed parsley to garnish

1 Heat a non-stick pan and fry the chicken thighs, skin side down, until golden. Turn over and fry for 5 minutes.

2 Add the onion and fry for 5 minutes. Add the tomatoes, mixed beans and vinegar, cover the pan and simmer for 10–12 minutes until piping hot. Garnish with parsley and serve immediately.

★ TRY SOMETHING DIFFERENT
Use flageolet beans or other canned beans instead of mixed beans, and garnish with fresh basil or oregano.

Lime and Chilli Chicken Goujons

Preparation Time 15 minutes • Cooking Time 20 minutes • Serves 4 • Per Serving 339 calories, 22g fat (of which 4g saturates), 22g carbohydrate, 1.9g salt • Easy

300g (11oz) boneless, skinless
  chicken thighs
50g (2oz) fresh breadcrumbs
50g (2oz) plain flour
2 tsp dried chilli flakes
grated zest of 1 lime
1 medium egg, beaten
2 tbsp sunflower oil
salt and ground black pepper
lime wedges to serve

FOR THE DIP
6 tbsp natural yogurt
6 tbsp mayonnaise
¼ cucumber, halved lengthways,
  seeded and finely diced
25g (1oz) freshly chopped coriander
juice of 1 lime

1 Put all the dip ingredients into a bowl. Season to taste with salt and pepper and mix well, then chill.

2 Cut the chicken into strips. Put the breadcrumbs into a bowl with the flour, chilli flakes, lime zest and 1 tsp salt and mix well. Pour the egg on to a plate. Dip the chicken in egg, then coat in the breadcrumbs.

3 Heat the oil in a frying pan over a medium heat. Fry the chicken in batches for 7–10 minutes until golden and cooked through. Keep each batch warm while cooking the remainder. Transfer to a serving plate, sprinkle with a little salt, then serve with the dip and lime wedges.

★ COOK'S TIP
For a lower-fat version, bake the goujons in the oven. Preheat the oven to 200°C (180°C fan oven) mark 6. Put the goujons on a lightly oiled baking sheet, brush each with a little oil and bake for 12–15 minutes until golden and cooked through.

Chilli Bean Cake

Preparation Time 10 minutes • Cooking Time 20 minutes • Serves 4 • Per Serving 265 calories, 6g fat (of which 1g saturates), 41g carbohydrate, 2.1g salt • Vegetarian • Dairy Free • Easy

3 tbsp olive oil

75g (3oz) wholemeal breadcrumbs

1 bunch of spring onions, finely chopped

1 orange pepper, seeded and chopped

1 small green chilli, seeded and finely chopped (see Cook's Tips, page 42)

1 garlic clove, crushed

1 tsp ground turmeric (optional)

400g can mixed beans, drained and rinsed

3 tbsp mayonnaise

a small handful of fresh basil, chopped

salt and ground black pepper

TO SERVE
soured cream
freshly chopped coriander
lime wedges (optional)

1 Heat 2 tbsp oil in a non-stick frying pan over a medium heat and fry the breadcrumbs until golden and beginning to crisp. Remove and put to one side.

2 Add the remaining oil to the pan and fry the spring onions until soft and golden. Add the orange pepper, chilli, garlic and turmeric, if using. Cook, stirring, for 5 minutes.

3 Tip in the beans, mayonnaise, two-thirds of the fried breadcrumbs and the basil. Season with salt and pepper, mash roughly with a fork, then press the mixture down to flatten and sprinkle with the remaining breadcrumbs. Fry the bean cake over a medium heat for 4–5 minutes until the base is golden. Remove from the heat, cut into wedges and serve with soured cream, coriander and the lime wedges, if you like.

Chilli Steak and Corn on the Cob

Preparation Time 5 minutes • Cooking Time 15 minutes • Serves 4 • Per Serving 564 calories, 31g fat (of which 14g saturates), 33g carbohydrate, 1.4g salt • Gluten Free • Easy

50g (2oz) butter, softened
1 large red chilli, seeded and finely
    chopped (see Cook's Tips,
    page 42)
1 garlic clove, crushed
25g (1oz) freshly grated Parmesan
1 tbsp finely chopped fresh basil
4 corn on the cob, each cut into
    three pieces
1 tbsp olive oil
4 sirloin steaks, about 150g (5oz)
    each
mixed green salad to serve

1 Put the butter into a bowl and beat with a wooden spoon. Add the chilli, garlic, Parmesan and basil and mix everything together. Cover and chill to firm up.

2 Meanwhile, bring a large pan of water to the boil. Add the corn, cover to bring back to the boil, then reduce the heat and simmer, half-covered, for about 10 minutes or until tender. Drain well.

3 Heat the oil in a large frying pan or griddle over a medium heat. Cook the steaks for 2–3 minutes on each side for medium-rare, or 3–4 minutes for medium.

4 Divide the corn and steaks among four warmed plates and top with the chilled butter. Serve immediately, with a mixed green salad.

Speedy Burgers

Preparation Time 10 minutes • Cooking Time 8–12 minutes • Serves 4 • Per Serving 80 calories, 20g fat (of which 8g saturates), 2g carbohydrate, 0.3g salt • Dairy Free • Gluten Free

450g (1lb) lean minced beef
1 onion, very finely chopped
1 tbsp dried Herbes de Provence
2 tsp sun-dried tomato paste
1 medium egg, beaten
ground black pepper
Chilli Coleslaw to serve (see
    Cook's Tip)

1 Put the minced beef, onion, herbs, tomato paste and beaten egg into a bowl and mix well. Season with pepper, then shape the mixture into four round burgers about 2cm (³⁄₄in) thick.

2 Preheat the grill or griddle pan. Cook the burgers for 4–6 minutes on each side and serve with chilli coleslaw.

★ COOK'S TIP
Chilli Coleslaw
Put 3 peeled and finely shredded carrots into a large bowl. Add ½ finely shredded white cabbage, 1 seeded and finely sliced red pepper and ½ chopped cucumber. Mix ½ tsp harissa paste with 100g (3½oz) natural yogurt and 1 tbsp white wine vinegar. Add to the vegetables and toss well.

Deli Pizza

Preparation Time 5 minutes • Cooking Time 15 minutes • Serves 4 • Per Serving 440 calories, 15g fat
(of which 5g saturates), 64g carbohydrate, 2.8g salt • Vegetarian • Easy

6 tbsp tomato pizza sauce
2 pizzeria-style pizza bases
100g (3½oz) soft goat's cheese
1 red onion, finely sliced
100g (3½oz) sunblush tomatoes
100g (3½oz) pitted black olives
a handful of fresh basil, roughly
   torn
green salad to serve

1 Preheat the oven to 220°C (200°C
fan oven) mark 7. Put a large baking
sheet on the top shelf to heat up.

2 Spread a thin layer of the tomato
sauce over each of the pizza bases,
leaving a 2.5cm (1in) border around
the edge. Top with dollops of goat's
cheese, then scatter the red onion,
tomatoes and olives over it.

3 Slide one of the pizzas on to the
hot baking sheet and bake for
15 minutes or until golden and
crisp. Repeat with the second pizza
base. Scatter the torn basil over

each pizza and serve immediately
with a green salad.

⭐ TRY SOMETHING
DIFFERENT
*Try marinated peppers, artichokes
or chargrilled aubergines instead of
the olives and sunblush tomatoes.*

Mozzarella, Parma Ham and Rocket Pizza

Preparation Time 10 minutes • Cooking Time 15–18 minutes • Serves 4 • Per Serving 508 calories, 19g fat (of which 11g saturates), 64g carbohydrate, 1.9g salt • Easy

a little plain flour to dust
290g pack pizza base mix
350g (12oz) fresh tomato and chilli pasta sauce
250g (9oz) buffalo mozzarella cheese, drained and roughly chopped
6 slices Parma ham, torn into strips
50g (2oz) rocket
a little extra virgin olive oil to drizzle
salt and ground black pepper

1 Preheat the oven to 200°C (180°C fan oven) mark 6. Lightly flour two large baking sheets. Mix up the pizza base according to the pack instructions. Divide the dough into two and knead each ball on a lightly floured surface for about 5 minutes, then roll them out to make two 23cm (9in) rounds. Put each on to a prepared baking sheet.

2 Divide the tomato sauce between the pizza bases and spread it over them, leaving a small border around the edge. Scatter on the mozzarella pieces, then scatter with ham. Season well with salt and pepper.

3 Cook the pizzas for 15–18 minutes until golden. Slide on to a wooden board, top with rocket leaves and drizzle with oil. Cut in half to serve.

⭐ COOK'S TIP
If you're short of time, buy two ready-made pizza bases.

Lamb with Butter Beans and Spinach

Preparation Time 5 minutes • Cooking Time 12–15 minutes • Serves 4 • Per Serving 489 calories, 25g fat (of which 8g saturates), 29g carbohydrate, 2.1g salt • Gluten Free • Easy

2 tbsp olive oil, plus extra to brush
1 onion, finely sliced
1 garlic clove, crushed
2 × 400g cans butter beans, drained
   and rinsed
200g (7oz) fresh spinach
4 small lamb chops
½ lemon, cut into wedges to serve

FOR THE DRESSING
3 tbsp low-fat natural yogurt
2 tbsp tahini (see Cook's Tips,
   page 86)
1 tsp harissa paste
juice of ½ lemon
salt and ground black pepper

1 Heat 1 tbsp oil in a large pan. Add the onion and fry over a medium heat for 10 minutes or until soft and golden. Add the garlic and cook for 1 minute, then add the butter beans and spinach and cook for 1–2 minutes to warm through and wilt the spinach.

2 Meanwhile, brush the lamb chops with a little oil and fry in a separate pan for 3–4 minutes on each side.

3 To make the dressing, put the remaining oil into a bowl and add the yogurt, tahini, harissa, lemon juice and 2 tbsp cold water. Season well and mix together.

4 To serve, divide the butter bean mixture among four warmed plates. Top each with a lamb chop, add a dollop of dressing and serve with the lemon wedges.

★ TRY SOMETHING DIFFERENT
Use cannellini or flageolet beans instead of butter beans.

Lamb Chops with Crispy Garlic Potatoes

Preparation Time 10 minutes • Cooking Time 20 minutes • Serves 4 • Per Serving 835 calories, 45g fat (of which 19g saturates), 22g carbohydrate, 0.7g salt • Gluten Free • Dairy Free • Easy.

2 tbsp Mint Sauce (see Cook's Tips)
8 small lamb chops
3 medium potatoes, cut into 5mm (¼in) slices
2 tbsp Garlic-infused Olive Oil (see Cook's Tips)
1 tbsp olive oil
salt and ground black pepper
steamed green beans to serve

1 Spread the mint sauce over the lamb chops and leave to marinate while you prepare the potatoes.

2 Boil the potatoes in a pan of lightly salted water for 2 minutes or until just starting to soften. Drain, tip back into the pan and season with salt and pepper, then add the garlic oil and toss to combine.

3 Meanwhile, heat the olive oil in a large frying pan and fry the chops for 4–5 minutes on each side until just cooked, adding a splash of boiling water to the pan to make a sauce. Remove the chops and sauce from the pan and keep warm.

4 Add the potatoes to the pan. Fry over a medium heat for 10–12 minutes until crisp and golden. Divide the potatoes, chops and sauce among four warmed plates and serve with green beans.

★ COOK'S TIPS

Mint Sauce
Finely chop 20g (¾oz) fresh mint and mix with 1 tbsp each olive oil and white wine vinegar.

Garlic-infused Olive Oil
Gently heat 2 tbsp olive oil with peeled sliced garlic for 5 minutes and use immediately. Do not store.

Flash-in-the-pan Pork

Preparation Time 5 minutes • Cooking Time 15 minutes • Serves 4 • Per Serving 346 calories, 12g fat (of which 4g saturates), 32g carbohydrate, 0.6g salt • Easy

700g (1½lb) new potatoes, scrubbed, halved if large
175g (6oz) runner beans, sliced
4 pork escalopes, about 150g (5oz) each
1 tbsp sunflower or olive oil
150ml (¼ pint) hot chicken stock
150ml (¼ pint) apple cider
2 tbsp wholegrain mustard
150g (5oz) Greek yogurt
4 fresh tarragon stems, leaves only
a squeeze of lemon juice
salt and ground black pepper

1 Cook the potatoes in a large pan of lightly salted boiling water for 10 minutes. Add the beans and cook for a further 5 minutes or until tender. Drain.

2 Meanwhile, season the escalopes with salt and pepper. Heat the oil in a large non-stick frying pan over a medium heat. Cook the pork for 3 minutes on each side or until browned. Remove from the pan and keep warm. Add the hot stock, cider and mustard to the pan and increase the heat to reduce the liquid by half.

3 Just before serving, reduce the heat and add the yogurt, tarragon leaves and lemon juice. Put the pork back into the pan to coat with the sauce and warm through. Serve with the potatoes and beans.

Quick Beef Stroganoff

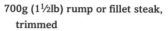

Preparation Time 10 minutes • Cooking Time 20 minutes • Serves 4 • Per Serving 750 calories, 60g fat
(of which 35g saturates), 3g carbohydrate, 0.5g salt • Gluten Free • Easy

700g (1½lb) rump or fillet steak,
   trimmed
50g (2oz) unsalted butter or 4 tbsp
   olive oil
1 onion, thinly sliced
225g (8oz) brown-cap mushrooms,
   sliced
3 tbsp brandy
1 tsp French mustard
200ml (7fl oz) crème fraîche
100ml (3½fl oz) double cream
3 tbsp freshly chopped flat-leafed
   parsley
salt and ground black pepper
rice or noodles to serve

1 Cut the steak into strips about 5mm (¼in) wide and 5cm (2in) long.

2 Heat half the butter or oil in a large heavy frying pan over a medium heat. Add the onion and cook gently for 10 minutes or until soft and golden. Remove with a slotted spoon and set aside. Add the mushrooms to the pan and cook, stirring, for 2–3 minutes until golden brown. Remove and set aside.

3 Increase the heat and and add the remaining butter or oil to the pan. Quickly fry the meat, in two or three batches, for 2–3 minutes, stirring constantly to ensure even browning. Add the brandy and allow it to bubble to reduce.

4 Put the meat, onion and mushrooms back into the pan. Reduce the heat and stir in the mustard, crème fraîche and cream. Heat through, stir in most of the parsley and season with salt and pepper. Serve with rice or noodles, with the remaining parsley scattered over the top.

 FREEZING TIP

To freeze Complete the recipe, transfer to a freezerproof container, cool, label and freeze for up to three months.
To use Thaw overnight in the fridge. Put into a pan, cover and bring to the boil, then reduce the heat to low and simmer until piping hot.

Quick Steak Supper

Preparation Time 10 minutes • Cooking Time 10 minutes • Serves 4 • Per Serving 452 calories, 17g fat (of which 6g saturates), 44g carbohydrate, 1.6g salt • Easy

2 sirloin steaks
3 tsp olive oil
4 large mushrooms, sliced
1 red onion, sliced
1 tbsp Dijon mustard
25g (1oz) butter
2 ciabattas, halved lengthways, then quartered, to make eight pieces
salt and ground black pepper
green salad to serve

1 Heat a griddle or large frying pan until very hot. Rub the steaks with 1 tsp oil, season with salt and pepper and fry for about 2 minutes on each side for rare, or 4 minutes each side for medium. Remove from the pan and leave to rest.

2 Heat the remaining oil in the pan. Add the mushrooms and red onion and fry, stirring, for 5 minutes or until softened. Stir in the Dijon mustard and butter and take off the heat.

3 Toast the ciabatta pieces on both sides. Thinly slice the steaks and divide among four pieces of ciabatta. Top with the mushrooms, onion and remaining ciabatta and serve with a green salad.

★ TRY SOMETHING DIFFERENT
Instead of ciabatta, serve the steak with tagliatelle or other pasta.

Speedy Beef Noodles

Preparation Time 5 minutes • Cooking Time 10 minutes • Serves 4 • Per Serving 510 calories, 19g fat (of which 5g saturates), 60g carbohydrate, 2.8g salt • Dairy Free • Easy

250g (9oz) fine egg noodles
4 tbsp sesame oil, plus a little extra
    to brush
300g (11oz) beef fillet
4 tbsp chilli soy sauce
juice of 1 lime
2 red peppers, halved, seeded and
    cut into thin strips
200g (7oz) mangetouts, sliced
4 tbsp freshly chopped coriander

1 Put the noodles into a large bowl and cover with boiling water. Leave to soak for 4 minutes, then rinse under cold running water and set aside.

2 Meanwhile, brush a large frying pan or griddle with a little oil and heat until hot. Fry the beef for 3–4 minutes on each side, or 4–5 minutes if you like it well done. Remove the meat from the pan and keep warm.

3 Add the 4 tbsp oil to the pan with the chilli soy sauce, lime juice, red peppers, mangetouts and coriander and stir to mix. Add the noodles and use two large spoons to toss them over the heat to combine with the sauce and warm through.

4 Cut the beef into thin slices and serve on a bed of noodles.

Pork Stir-fry with Chilli and Mango

Preparation Time 5 minutes • Cooking Time about 10 minutes • Serves 4 • Per Serving 138 calories, 4g fat
(of which 1g saturates), 17g carbohydrate, 0.8g salt • Dairy Free • Easy

75g (3oz) medium egg noodles
1 tsp groundnut oil
½ red chilli, seeded and finely
    chopped (see Cook's Tips, here
    and on page 42)
125g (4oz) pork stir-fry strips
1 head pak choi, roughly chopped
1 tbsp soy sauce
½ ripe mango, peeled, stoned and
    sliced

1 Cook the noodles in boiling water according to the pack instructions. Drain, then plunge them into cold water and put to one side.

2 Meanwhile, heat the oil in a wok or large frying pan until very hot. Add the chilli and pork and stir-fry for 3–4 minutes. Add the pak choi and soy sauce and cook for a further 2–3 minutes. Add the mango and toss to combine.

3 Drain the noodles and add them to the pan. Toss well and cook for 1–2 minutes until heated through. Serve immediately.

★ COOK'S TIP
The smaller the chilli, the hotter it is.

Turkey and Sesame Stir-fry with Noodles

Preparation Time 5 minutes, plus marinating • Cooking Time 10 minutes • Serves 4 • Per Serving 672 calories, 18g fat (of which 4g saturates), 97g carbohydrate, 0.7g salt • Dairy Free • Easy

300g (11oz) turkey breast fillets, cut into thin strips
3 tbsp teriyaki marinade
3 tbsp clear honey
500g (1lb 2oz) medium egg noodles
about 1 tbsp sesame oil, plus extra for the noodles
300g (11oz) ready-prepared mixed stir-fry vegetables, such as carrots, broccoli, red cabbage, mangetouts, bean sprouts and purple spring onions
2 tbsp sesame seeds, lightly toasted in a dry wok or heavy-based pan

1 Put the turkey strips into a large bowl with the teriyaki marinade and honey and stir to coat. Cover and set aside for 5 minutes.

2 Cook the noodles in boiling water for about 4 minutes or according to the pack instructions. Drain well, then toss in a little oil.

3 Heat 1 tbsp oil in a wok or large frying pan and add the turkey, reserving the marinade. Stir-fry over a very high heat for 2–3 minutes until cooked through and beginning to brown. Add a drop more oil, if needed, then add the vegetables and reserved marinade. Continue to cook over a high heat, stirring, until the vegetables have started to soften and the sauce is warmed through.

4 Scatter with the sesame seeds and serve immediately with the noodles.

Spiced Tikka Kebabs

Preparation Time 10 minutes • Cooking Time 20 minutes • Serves 4 • Per Serving 150 calories, 5g fat
(of which 1g saturates), 4g carbohydrate, 0.3g salt • Gluten Free • Easy

2 tbsp tikka paste
150g (5oz) natural yogurt
juice of ½ lime
4 spring onions, chopped
350g (12oz) skinless chicken, cut
   into bite-size pieces
lime wedges and Mixed Salad (see
   Cook's Tip) to serve

1 Preheat the grill. Put the tikka paste, yogurt, lime juice and spring onions into a large bowl. Add the chicken and toss well. Thread the chicken on to metal skewers.

2 Grill the chicken for 8–10 minutes on each side, turning and basting with the paste, until cooked through. Serve with lime wedges to squeeze over the kebabs, and mixed salad.

★ COOK'S TIP
Mixed Salad
Put 75g (3oz) green salad leaves into a large bowl. Add ¼ chopped avocado, a handful of halved cherry tomatoes, ½ chopped cucumber and the juice of 1 lime. Season to taste with salt and pepper and mix together.

Chicken, Bean and Spinach Curry

Preparation Time 10 minutes • Cooking Time about 20 minutes • Serves 4 • Per Serving 364 calories, 9g fat
(of which 1g saturates), 41g carbohydrate, 2.9g salt • Gluten Free • Easy

1 tbsp sunflower oil
350g (12oz) boneless, skinless
  chicken breasts, cut into strips
1 garlic clove, crushed
300–350g tub or jar curry sauce
400g can aduki beans, drained and
  rinsed
175g (6oz) ready-to-eat dried
  apricots
150g (5oz) natural bio yogurt, plus
  extra to serve
125g (4oz) baby spinach leaves
naan bread to serve

1 Heat the oil in a large pan over a medium heat and fry the chicken strips with the garlic until golden. Add the curry sauce, beans and apricots, then cover and simmer gently for 15 minutes or until the chicken is tender.

2 Over a low heat, stir in the yogurt, keeping the curry hot without boiling it, then stir in the spinach until it just begins to wilt. Add a spoonful of yogurt and serve with naan bread.

★ TRY SOMETHING DIFFERENT
Use pork escalopes, cut into thin strips, instead of chicken.

Quick Chicken Stir-fry

Preparation Time 10 minutes • Cooking Time 12 minutes • Serves 4 • Per Serving 316 calories, 3g fat (of which 1g saturates), 46g carbohydrate, 0.5g salt • Gluten Free • Dairy Free • Easy

1 tsp groundnut oil
300g (11oz) boneless, skinless chicken breasts, sliced
4 spring onions, chopped
200g (7oz) medium rice noodles
100g (3½oz) mangetouts
200g (7oz) purple sprouting broccoli, chopped
2–3 tbsp sweet chilli sauce
freshly chopped coriander and lime wedges (optional) to garnish

1 Heat the oil in a wok or large frying pan. Add the chicken and spring onions and stir-fry over a high heat for 5–6 minutes until the chicken is golden.

2 Meanwhile, soak the rice noodles in boiling water for 4 minutes or according to the pack instructions.

3 Add the mangetouts, broccoli and chilli sauce to the chicken. Continue to stir-fry for 4 minutes.

4 Drain the noodles, then add to the pan and toss everything together. Scatter the chopped coriander over the top and serve with lime wedges to squeeze over the stir-fry, if you like.

⭐ TRY SOMETHING DIFFERENT
Other vegetables are just as good in this dish: try pak choi, button mushrooms, carrots cut into matchsticks, or baby sweetcorn.

Chicken Chow Mein

Preparation Time 10 minutes • Cooking Time 10 minutes • Serves 4 • Per Serving 451 calories, 11g fat (of which 2g saturates), 59g carbohydrate, 1.3g salt • Dairy Free • Easy

250g (9oz) medium egg noodles
1 tbsp toasted sesame oil
2 boneless, skinless chicken
  breasts, about 125g (4oz) each,
  cut into thin strips
1 bunch of spring onions, thinly
  sliced diagonally
150g (5oz) mangetouts, thickly
  sliced diagonally
125g (4oz) bean sprouts
100g (3½oz) cooked ham, finely
  shredded
120g sachet chow mein sauce
salt and ground black pepper
light soy sauce to serve

1 Cook the noodles in boiling water for 4 minutes or according to the pack instructions. Drain, rinse thoroughly in cold water, drain again and set aside.

2 Meanwhile, heat a wok or large frying pan until hot, then add the oil. Add the chicken and stir-fry over a high heat for 3–4 minutes until browned all over. Add the spring onions and mangetouts and stir-fry for 2 minutes. Stir in the bean sprouts and ham and cook for a further 2 minutes.

3 Add the drained noodles, then pour the chow mein sauce into the pan and toss together to coat evenly. Stir-fry for 2 minutes or until piping hot. Season with salt and pepper and serve immediately with light soy sauce to drizzle over the chow mein.

Fish Suppers

Fast Fish Soup

Preparation Time 10 minutes • Cooking Time 15 minutes • Serves 4 • Per Serving 269 calories, 10g fat (of which 2g saturates), 6g carbohydrate, 0.6g salt • Gluten Free • Dairy Free • Easy

1 leek, trimmed and finely sliced
4 fat garlic cloves, crushed
3 celery sticks, finely sliced
1 small fennel bulb, finely sliced
1 red chilli, seeded and finely
chopped (see Cook's Tips, page 42)
3 tbsp olive oil
50ml (2fl oz) dry white wine
about 750g (1lb 10oz) mixed fish and shellfish, such as haddock, monkfish and salmon, raw shelled prawns, and mussels, scrubbed, rinsed and beards removed (see Cook's Tip, page 155)

4 medium tomatoes, chopped
1½ tbsp freshly chopped thyme
salt and ground black pepper

1 Put the leek into a large pan and add the garlic, celery, fennel, chilli and oil. Cook over a medium heat for 5 minutes or until the vegetables are soft and beginning to colour.

2 Stir in 1.1 litres (2 pints) boiling water and the wine. Bring to the boil, then reduce the heat, cover and simmer for 5 minutes.

3 Meanwhile, cut the white fish into large chunks. Add to the soup with the tomatoes and thyme. Continue to simmer gently until the fish has just turned opaque. Add the prawns and simmer for 1 minute, then add the mussels. As soon as all the mussels have opened, season the soup and ladle into warmed bowls. Discard any mussels that remain closed, then serve immediately.

★ COOK'S TIP
Frozen seafood mix is a useful standby. Use it instead of the fish and shellfish in this recipe but take care not to overcook or it will become tough.

★ TRY SOMETHING DIFFERENT
● *To give the soup more of a kick, stir in 2 tbsp Pernod instead of the wine.*
● *Garlic croûtes are traditionally served with fish soup; they can be made while the soup is simmering. Toast small slices of baguette, spread with garlic mayonnaise and sprinkle with grated cheese. Float in the hot soup just before serving.*

Chinese-style Fish

Preparation Time 5 minutes • Cooking Time 10 minutes • Serves 4 • Per Serving 150 calories, 3g fat
(of which 1g saturates), 10g carbohydrate, 0.7g salt • Gluten Free • Dairy Free • Easy

2 tsp sunflower oil
1 small onion, finely chopped
1 green chilli, seeded and finely
    chopped (see Cook's Tips,
    page 42)
2 courgettes, thinly sliced
125g (4oz) frozen peas, thawed
350g (12oz) skinless haddock fillet,
    cut into bite-size pieces
2 tsp lemon juice
4 tbsp hoisin sauce
lime wedges to serve

1 Heat the oil in a large non-stick frying pan. Add the onion, chilli, courgettes and peas and stir-fry over a high heat for 5 minutes or until the onion and courgettes begin to soften.

2 Add the fish to the pan with the lemon juice, hoisin sauce and 150ml (¼ pint) water. Bring to the boil, then reduce the heat and simmer, uncovered, for 2–3 minutes until the fish is cooked through. Serve with lime wedges.

★ TRY SOMETHING DIFFERENT
There are plenty of alternatives to haddock: try sea bass, sea bream or gurnard.

Cod with Sweet Chilli Glaze

Preparation Time 10 minutes • Cooking Time 20 minutes • Serves 4 • Per Serving 193 calories, 1g fat (of which trace saturates), 13g carbohydrate, 0.7g salt • Gluten Free • Easy

1 red chilli, seeded and finely chopped (see Cook's Tips, page 42)

2 tsp dark soy sauce

grated zest and juice of 1 lime

¼ tsp ground allspice or 6 allspice berries, crushed

50g (2oz) light muscovado sugar

4 thick cod fillets, with skin, about 175g (6oz) each

finely sliced red chilli, finely sliced lime zest and lime wedges to garnish

FOR THE SAFFRON MASH

900g (2lb) potatoes, roughly chopped

a pinch of saffron threads

50g (2oz) butter

salt and ground black pepper

1 To make the saffron mash, cook the potatoes in lightly salted boiling water until tender. Meanwhile, soak the saffron in 2 tbsp boiling water. Drain the potatoes and mash with the butter, then beat in the saffron liquid. Season to taste with salt and pepper.

2 Meanwhile, preheat the grill or griddle pan until hot. Stir the chopped chilli, soy sauce, lime zest and juice, allspice and sugar together.

3 Grill the cod for about 1 minute on the flesh side. Turn skin side up and grill for 1 minute. Spoon the chilli glaze over the fish and grill for a further 2–3 minutes until the skin is crisp and golden.

4 Garnish with finely sliced chilli and lime zest and the lime wedges. Serve with the saffron mash.

 TRY SOMETHING DIFFERENT

Use sea bass, gurnard, coley (saithe) or pollack instead of the cod.

Crusted Trout

Preparation Time 10 minutes • Cooking Time 10–13 minutes • Serves 4 • Per Serving 259 calories, 15g fat (of which 3g saturates), 1g carbohydrate, 0.8g salt • Gluten Free • Dairy Free • Easy

1 tbsp sesame oil
1 tbsp soy sauce
juice of 1 lime
4 × 150g (5oz) trout fillets
2 tbsp sesame seeds
lime wedges, herb salad and fennel
to serve

1 Preheat the grill. Put the oil into a bowl, add the soy sauce and lime juice and whisk together.

2 Put the trout fillets on a baking sheet, pour the sesame mixture over them and grill for 8–10 minutes. Sprinkle with the sesame seeds and grill for a further 2–3 minutes until the seeds are golden. Serve with lime wedges, a herb salad and some finely sliced fennel.

⭐ COOK'S TIP
Sesame seeds are deliciously nutty and highly nutritious. They are a valuable source of protein, good omega fats and vitamin E. Lightly toasted sesame seeds, crushed with a little salt and stirred into 1–2 tbsp olive oil, make an excellent dressing for cooked green beans, broccoli and carrots.

Trout with Apple and Watercress Salad

Preparation Time 15 minutes • Cooking Time 15–20 minutes • Serves 4 • Per Serving 320 calories, 12g fat (of which 1g saturates), 21g carbohydrate, 0.4g salt • Gluten Free • Dairy Free • Easy

4 × 150g (5oz) trout fillets
1 tbsp olive oil, plus extra to grease
250g (9oz) cooked baby new
    potatoes, cut into chunks
2 apples, cored and cut into chunks
4 cooked beetroot in natural juice,
    cut into chunks
150g (5oz) watercress
salt and ground black pepper

FOR THE DRESSING
1 tbsp extra virgin olive oil
juice of ½ lemon
2 tsp Dijon mustard
1 tbsp freshly chopped dill

1 Preheat the oven to 200°C (180°C fan oven) mark 6. Put each piece of fish on a piece of greased foil, brush the top of the fish with olive oil and season with salt and pepper. Scrunch the foil around the fish and roast for 15–20 minutes until the fish is cooked.

2 Put the potatoes, apples, beetroot and watercress into a large bowl and mix lightly.

3 Mix all the dressing ingredients together in a small bowl and season with salt and pepper. Add to the salad and toss through, then serve with the fish.

Crispy Crumbed Fish

Preparation Time 5 minutes • Cooking Time 10–15 minutes • Serves 4 • Per Serving 171 calories, 1g fat (of which trace saturates), 10g carbohydrate, 0.8g salt • Dairy Free • Easy

50g (2oz) fresh breadcrumbs
a small handful of freshly chopped
flat-leafed parsley
2 tbsp capers, chopped
grated zest of 1 lemon
4 haddock or pollack fillets, about
150g (5oz) each
½ tbsp Dijon mustard
juice of ½ lemon
salt and ground black pepper
new potatoes and mixed salad
to serve

1 Preheat the oven to 180°C (160°C fan oven) mark 4. Put the breadcrumbs into a bowl with the parsley, capers and lemon zest. Mix well, then set aside.

2 Put the fish fillets on a baking tray. Mix the mustard and half the lemon juice in a bowl with a little salt and pepper, then spread over the top of each piece of fish. Spoon the breadcrumb mixture on top – don't worry if some falls off.

3 Cook in the oven for 10–15 minutes until the fish is cooked and the breadcrumbs are golden. Pour the remaining lemon juice over the top and serve with new potatoes and a mixed salad.

Quick Fish and Chips

Preparation Time 15 minutes • Cooking Time 12 minutes • Serves 2 • Per Serving 1186 calories, 79g fat (of which 18g saturates), 73g carbohydrate, 3.2g salt • Dairy Free • Easy

4 litres (7 pints) sunflower oil for deep-frying
125g (4oz) self-raising flour
¼ tsp baking powder
¼ tsp salt
1 medium egg
150ml (¼ pint) sparkling mineral water
2 hake fillets, about 125g (4oz) each
450g (1lb) Desirée potatoes, cut into 1cm (½in) chips
salt, vinegar and garlic mayonnaise to serve

1 Heat the oil in a deep-fryer to 190°C (test by frying a small cube of bread – it should brown in 20 seconds).

2 Whiz the flour, baking powder, salt, egg and water in a food processor until combined into a batter. Remove the blade from the food processor. Alternatively, put the ingredients into a bowl and beat everything together until smooth. Drop one of the fish fillets into the batter to coat it.

3 Put half the chips in the deep-fryer, then add the battered fish. Fry for 6 minutes or until just cooked, then remove and drain well on kitchen paper. Keep warm if not serving immediately.

4 Drop the remaining fillet into the batter to coat, then repeat step 3 with the remaining chips. Serve with salt, vinegar and garlic mayonnaise.

Thai Fishcakes with Chilli Mayo

Preparation Time 25 minutes • Cooking Time 8–10 minutes • Serves 4 • Per Serving 554 calories, 44g fat (of which 6g saturates), 17g carbohydrate, 1.3g salt • Dairy Free • Easy

1 bunch of spring onions
2.5cm (1in) piece fresh root ginger, peeled and roughly chopped
1 lemongrass stalk, roughly chopped
20g pack fresh coriander
½ red chilli, seeded (see Cook's Tips, page 42), plus strips of red chilli to garnish
1 tsp Thai fish sauce (optional)
150ml (¼ pint) mayonnaise
75g (3oz) fresh white breadcrumbs
225g (8oz) haddock
225g (8oz) cooked and peeled prawns

oil for frying
2 tbsp Thai sweet chilli sauce
20g pack fresh basil, roughly chopped
1 fat garlic clove, crushed (optional)
2 limes, cut into wedges, and 120g bag baby leaf spinach to serve

1 Put the spring onions, ginger, lemongrass, coriander, chilli and fish sauce, if using, into a food processor and whiz to a rough paste. Add 3 tbsp mayonnaise, the breadcrumbs, haddock and prawns and whiz for 5 seconds.

2 With wet hands, shape the mixture into eight patties, each about 5cm (2in) in diameter.

3 Heat a drizzle of oil in a non-stick frying pan. Fry the patties, in two batches, for 3–4 minutes on each side until crisp and golden.

4 Mix the sweet chilli sauce, basil and garlic, if using, into the remaining mayonnaise.

5 Serve the fishcakes garnished with red chilli strips, with lime wedges, the chilli mayo and spinach leaves.

Simple Smoked Haddock

Preparation Time 10 minutes • Cooking Time 10 minutes • Serves 4 • Per Serving 217 calories, 9g fat (of which 4g saturates), 1g carbohydrate, 3.4g salt • Gluten Free • Easy

25g (1oz) unsalted butter
1 tbsp olive oil
1 garlic clove, thinly sliced
4 thick smoked haddock or cod
    fillets, about 175g (6oz) each
a small handful of freshly chopped
    parsley (optional)
finely grated zest of 1 small lemon,
plus lemon wedges to serve
    (optional)
romanesco, cauliflower or broccoli
    to serve

1 Heat the butter, oil and garlic in a large non-stick pan over a high heat until the mixture starts to foam and sizzle. Put the fish into the pan, skin side down, and fry for 10 minutes – this will give a golden crust underneath the fish.

2 Turn the fish over. Scatter the parsley, if using, and lemon zest over each fillet, then fry for a further 30 seconds.

3 Put a cooked fillet on each of four warmed plates and spoon some of the buttery juices over them. Serve with lemon wedges, if using, and steamed romanesco, cauliflower or broccoli.

★ COOK'S TIP
Smoked fish is quite salty so always taste the sauce before seasoning with any extra salt.

Pesto Cod with Butter Beans

Preparation Time 5 minutes • Cooking Time 15 minutes • Serves 4 • Per Serving 403 calories, 16g fat (of which 3g saturates), 24g carbohydrate, 2.5g salt • Gluten Free • Easy

4 cod fillets, about 150g (5oz) each
4 tbsp red pepper pesto
2 tbsp olive oil
2 × 400g cans butter beans, drained
   and rinsed
2 garlic cloves, crushed
225g (8oz) fresh spinach
lemon juice
salt and ground black pepper
lemon juice to serve

1 Preheat the grill to medium. Spread each cod fillet evenly with 1 tbsp pesto and grill for 10–15 minutes until the flesh is opaque and just cooked.

2 Meanwhile, heat the oil in a pan and add the butter beans and garlic. Cook for 10 minutes, stirring occasionally and mashing the beans lightly as they warm through. Season with salt and pepper.

3 About 2–3 minutes before serving, add the spinach to the pan and allow it to wilt. Spoon the butter beans on to four warmed plates and top with the cod and any juices from grilling. Squeeze a little lemon juice over each piece of fish and serve immediately.

Grilled Sardines with Harissa

Preparation Time 10 minutes • Cooking Time 10–20 minutes • Serves 2 • Per Serving 292 calories, 21g fat (of which 4g saturates), 2g carbohydrate, 0.3g salt • Gluten Free • Dairy Free • Easy

1 garlic clove, crushed
2 tbsp olive oil
1–2 tsp harissa paste
4 whole sardines
salt and ground black pepper
tomato salad, watercress and lime
   wedges to serve

1 Preheat the grill to high. Put the garlic in a bowl. Add the oil and harissa, season to taste with salt and pepper and mix well.

2 Slash the sardines a couple of times on each side, then brush the harissa and oil mixture all over them. Grill for 5–10 minutes on each side until cooked through.

3 Serve with tomato salad and watercress, with lime wedges to squeeze over the sardines.

★ COOK'S TIP
Oily fish such as sardines are one of the best sources of heart-protecting omega-3 oils. Eat them at least once a week. Fresh Cornish sardines, when they are available, are a treat and are cheap. Look out for them at your fishmonger's or on the fresh fish counter at the supermarket.

Peppered Mackerel

Preparation Time 10 minutes • Cooking Time 15 minutes • Serves 4 • Per Serving 764 calories, 63g fat (of which 22g saturates), 1g carbohydrate, 0.4g salt • Gluten Free • Easy

4 tsp whole mixed peppercorns
4 fresh mackerel, gutted, about
   250g (9oz) each
1 tbsp sunflower oil
200ml (7fl oz) crème fraîche
lemon wedges to garnish
asparagus and sugarsnap peas
   to serve

1 Lightly crush 2 tsp peppercorns using a pestle and mortar. Sprinkle one side of each mackerel with half the crushed peppercorns.

2 Heat the oil in a frying pan over a medium-high heat. Add the fish, peppered side down, and cook for 5–7 minutes. Sprinkle the mackerel with the remaining crushed peppercorns, turn the fish over and continue to fry for 5–7 minutes until cooked (see Cook's Tips). Remove and keep warm.

3 Wipe out the pan, add the crème fraîche and bring to the boil. Stir in the remaining whole peppercorns. (If the sauce becomes too thick, add some boiling water.)

4 To serve, spoon the sauce over the mackerel, garnish with lemon wedges and serve with asparagus and sugarsnap peas.

★ COOK'S TIPS
● *If the mackerel are large, make three shallow slashes on either side of the fish.*
● *To test whether the fish is cooked, prise the flesh from the backbone with a knife: it should be opaque and come away easily.*

Tuna Melt Pizza

Preparation Time 5 minutes • Cooking Time 10–12 minutes • Serves 4 • Per Serving 688 calories, 26g fat (of which 9g saturates), 72g carbohydrate, 3.5g salt • Easy

2 large pizza bases
4 tbsp sun-dried tomato pesto
2 × 185g cans tuna, drained
50g can anchovies, drained and chopped
125g (4oz) mature Cheddar, grated
rocket to serve

1 Preheat the oven to 220°C (200°C fan oven) mark 7. Spread each pizza base with 2 tbsp sun-dried tomato pesto. Top each with half the tuna, half the anchovies and half the grated cheese.

2 Put on to a baking sheet and cook in the oven for 10–12 minutes until the cheese has melted. Sprinkle with rocket to serve.

★ TRY SOMETHING DIFFERENT

Mozzarella and Tomato Pizza
Spread the pizza bases with 4 tbsp pesto and top with 125g (4oz) chopped sunblush tomatoes and 2 x 125g sliced mozzarella balls. Cook, then serve topped with a handful of baby spinach leaves.

Ham and Pineapple Pizza
Spread the pizza bases with 4 tbsp tomato pasta sauce. Top with a 225g can drained unsweetened pineapple chunks, 125g (4oz) diced ham and 125g (4oz) grated Gruyère.

Simple Salmon Pasta

Preparation Time 2 minutes • Cooking Time 8 minutes • Serves 4 • Per Serving 630 calories, 13g fat (of which 6g saturates), 101g carbohydrate, 2.7g salt • Easy

500g (1lb 2oz) linguine pasta
a little olive oil
1 fat garlic clove, crushed
200ml (7fl oz) half-fat crème fraîche
225g (8oz) hot-smoked salmon,
    flaked
200g (7oz) peas
2 handfuls of fresh basil, roughly
    torn, to garnish
salt and ground black pepper

1 Cook the pasta in a large pan of lightly salted boiling water according to the pack instructions, then drain, reserving a couple of tablespoons of the cooking water.

2 Meanwhile, heat the oil in a large pan, add the garlic and fry gently until golden. Add the crème fraîche, salmon and peas and stir in. Cook for 1–2 minutes until warmed through, then add the reserved water from the pasta.

3 Toss the pasta in the sauce, season with salt and pepper and serve garnished with the torn basil.

 COOK'S TIP
Adding the reserved pasta cooking water stops the pasta absorbing too much of the crème fraîche.

Stir-fried Salmon and Broccoli

Preparation Time 10 minutes • Cooking Time 5–6 minutes • Serves 2 • Per Serving 90 calories, 4g fat (of which 1g saturates), 9g carbohydrate, 2.7g salt • Dairy Free • Easy

2 tsp sesame oil
1 red pepper, seeded and thinly
  sliced
½ red chilli, seeded and thinly
  sliced (see Cook's Tips, page 42)
1 garlic clove, crushed
125g (4oz) broccoli florets
2 spring onions, sliced
2 salmon fillets, about 125g (4oz)
  each, cut into strips
1 tsp Thai fish sauce
2 tsp soy sauce
wholewheat noodles to serve

1 Heat the oil in a wok or large frying pan. Add the red pepper, chilli, garlic, broccoli florets and spring onions and stir-fry over a high heat for 3–4 minutes.

2 Add the salmon, fish sauce and soy sauce and cook for 2 minutes, stirring gently. Serve immediately with wholewheat noodles.

Five-minute Stir-fry

Preparation Time 2 minutes • Cooking Time 5 minutes • Serves 2 • Per Serving 170 calories, 7g fat (of which 1g saturates), 11g carbohydrate, 1.6g salt • Gluten Free • Dairy Free • Easy

1 tbsp sesame oil
175g (6oz) raw peeled tiger prawns, deveined (see page 93)
50ml (2fl oz) ready-made sweet chilli and ginger sauce
225g (8oz) ready-prepared mixed stir-fry vegetables, such as sliced courgettes, broccoli and green beans

1 Heat the oil in a large wok or frying pan, add the prawns and sweet chilli and ginger sauce and stir-fry for 2 minutes.

2 Add the mixed vegetables and stir-fry for a further 2–3 minutes until the prawns are cooked and the vegetables are heated through. Serve immediately.

★ TRY SOMETHING DIFFERENT
Instead of prawns, try chicken cut into strips: stir-fry for 5 minutes in step 1.

Ginger, Leek and Prawn Stir-fry

Preparation Time 10 minutes • Cooking Time 15 minutes • Serves 4 • Per Serving 152 calories, 3g fat (of which 1g saturates), 10g carbohydrate, 1.2g salt • Gluten Free • Dairy Free • Easy

2 tsp olive oil
1 bunch of spring onions, chopped
1 garlic clove, crushed
2.5cm (1in) piece fresh root ginger, peeled and grated
3 leeks, trimmed and roughly chopped
1 red pepper, seeded and roughly chopped
400g (14oz) cooked prawns
1 tbsp tamari (wheat-free Japanese soy sauce)
2 tsp tomato purée, diluted in 1 tbsp water
1 tsp runny honey
ground black pepper
rice or quinoa to serve

1 Heat the oil in a pan, add the spring onions, garlic, ginger and 2 tbsp water and fry for 2 minutes over a medium heat. Add the leeks and red pepper and stir-fry for 10 minutes or until softened.

2 Add the prawns, tamari, tomato purée and honey to the pan. Season with pepper and cook for 30 seconds to 1 minute, stirring. Serve with rice or quinoa.

⭐ TRY SOMETHING DIFFERENT
Use scallops instead of the prawns. Alternatively, use any firm-textured white fish, such as monkfish, discarding the skin and cutting the fish into small cubes.

Prawn and Peanut Noodles

Preparation Time 10 minutes, plus soaking • Serves 4 • Per Serving 579 calories, 24g fat (of which 7g saturates), 67g carbohydrate, 0.7g salt • Dairy Free • Easy

300g (11oz) straight-to-wok noodles
360g pack stir-fry vegetables
4 tbsp coconut cream
4 tbsp smooth peanut butter
1 tbsp Thai red or green curry paste
juice of ½ lime
225g (8oz) cooked and peeled king prawns
a small handful of freshly chopped coriander
25g (1oz) peanuts, chopped

1 Put the noodles and stir-fry vegetables into a large bowl or wok and cover with boiling water. Cover with clingfilm and leave for 5 minutes.

2 Meanwhile, mix the coconut cream with the peanut butter, curry paste and lime juice in a bowl.

3 Drain the noodles and vegetables in a colander. Put back into the bowl and toss with the prawns, coriander and half the dressing. Sprinkle with the peanuts and serve with the remaining dressing.

★ COOK'S TIP
Ready-prepared stir-fry vegetables make this extra-quick, but if you can't find them, try a mixture of three or four of the following: strips of red, orange or yellow peppers, baby sweetcorn, mangetouts or sugarsnaps, carrots cut into matchsticks, bean sprouts.

Penne with Smoked Salmon

Preparation Time 5 minutes • Cooking Time 10–15 minutes • Serves 4 • Per Serving 432 calories, 11g fat (of which 6g saturates), 67g carbohydrate, 1.7g salt • Easy

350g (12oz) penne or other short tubular pasta
200ml (7fl oz) half-fat crème fraîche
150g (5oz) smoked salmon, roughly chopped
20g (¾oz) fresh dill, finely chopped
salt and ground black pepper
lemon wedges to serve (optional)

1 Cook the pasta in a large pan of lightly salted boiling water according to the pack instructions. Drain.

2 Meanwhile, put the crème fraîche into a large bowl. Add the smoked salmon and dill, season well with salt and pepper and mix together. Gently stir into the drained penne and serve immediately with lemon wedges, if you like, to squeeze over the salmon and pasta.

Prawn and Vegetable Pilau

Preparation Time 10 minutes • Cooking Time 15–20 minutes • Serves 4 • Per Serving 360 calories, 5g fat (of which 1g saturates), 61g carbohydrate, 1.8g salt • Dairy Free • Easy

250g (9oz) long-grain rice
1 broccoli head, broken into florets
150g (5oz) baby sweetcorn, halved
200g (7oz) sugarsnap peas
1 red pepper, seeded and sliced into thin strips
400g (14oz) cooked and peeled king prawns

FOR THE DRESSING
1 tbsp sesame oil
5cm (2in) piece fresh root ginger, peeled and grated
juice of 1 lime
1–2 tbsp light soy sauce

1 Put the rice into a large wide pan – it needs to be really big, as you'll be cooking the rice and steaming the vegetables on top, then tossing it all together. Add 600ml (1 pint) boiling water. Cover and bring to the boil, then reduce the heat to low and cook the rice according to the pack instructions.

2 About 10 minutes before the end of the rice cooking time, add the broccoli, corn, sugarsnaps and red pepper. Stir well, then cover the pan and cook until the vegetables and rice are just tender.

3 Meanwhile, put the prawns into a bowl. Add the sesame oil, ginger, lime and soy sauce. Mix the prawns and dressing into the cooked vegetables and rice and toss well. Serve immediately.

⭐ COOK'S TIP
The word 'pilau', or 'pilaf', comes from the Persian 'pilaw'. The dish consists of rice flavoured with spices, to which vegetables, poultry, meat, fish or shellfish are added.

Simple Fried Rice

Preparation Time 5 minutes • Cooking Time 15–20 minutes • Serves 4 • Per Serving 339 calories, 11g fat (of which 2g saturates), 37g carbohydrate, 0.4g salt • Gluten Free • Dairy Free • Easy

150g (5oz) long-grain rice
2 tbsp sesame oil
3 medium eggs, lightly beaten
250g (9oz) frozen petits pois
250g (9oz) cooked and peeled
  prawns

1 Cook the rice in boiling water for about 10 minutes or according to the pack instructions. Drain well.

2 Heat 1 tsp oil in a large non-stick frying pan. Pour in half the beaten eggs and tilt the pan around over the heat for about 1 minute until the egg is set. Tip the omelette on to a warm plate. Repeat with another 1 tsp oil and the remaining beaten egg to make another omelette. Tip on to another warm plate.

3 Add the remaining oil to the pan and stir in the rice and peas. Stir-fry for 2–3 minutes until the peas are cooked. Stir in the prawns.

4 Roll up the omelettes, roughly chop one-third of one, then slice the remainder into strips. Add the chopped omelette to the rice, peas and prawns and cook for 1–2 minutes until heated through. Divide the fried rice among four bowls, top with the sliced omelette and serve immediately.

Quick Pad Thai

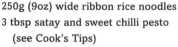

Preparation Time 12 minutes, plus soaking • Cooking Time 8 minutes • Serves 4 • Per Serving 451 calories, 13g fat (of which 3g saturates), 56g carbohydrate, 2.6g salt • Dairy Free • Easy

250g (9oz) wide ribbon rice noodles

3 tbsp satay and sweet chilli pesto (see Cook's Tips)

125g (4oz) mangetouts, thinly sliced

125g (4oz) sugarsnap peas, thinly sliced

3 medium eggs, beaten

3 tbsp chilli soy sauce, plus extra to serve (see Cook's Tips)

250g (9oz) cooked and peeled tiger prawns

25g (1oz) dry-roasted peanuts, roughly crushed

lime wedges to serve (optional)

1 Put the noodles into a heatproof bowl, cover with boiling water and soak for 4 minutes until softened. Drain, rinse under cold water and set aside.

2 Heat a wok or large frying pan until hot, add the chilli pesto and stir-fry for 1 minute. Add the mangetouts and sugarsnap peas and cook for a further 2 minutes. Tip into a bowl. Put the pan back on the heat, add the eggs and cook, stirring, for 1 minute.

3 Add the soy sauce, prawns and noodles to the pan. Toss well and cook for 3 minutes or until piping hot. Return the vegetables to the pan and cook for a further 1 minute until heated through, then sprinkle with the peanuts. Serve with extra soy sauce, and lime wedges to squeeze over the pad Thai, if you like.

★ COOK'S TIPS

● *If you can't find satay and sweet chilli pesto, substitute 2 tbsp peanut butter and 1 tbsp sweet chilli sauce.*

● *Chilli soy sauce can be replaced with 2 tbsp light soy sauce and ½ red chilli, finely chopped (see Cook's Tips, page 42).*

Mussel and Potato Stew

Preparation Time 15 minutes • Cooking Time 15 minutes • Serves 4 • Per Serving 470 calories, 23g fat (of which 11g saturates), 42g carbohydrate, 2.8g salt • Gluten Free • Easy

25g (1oz) butter
200g (7oz) rindless back bacon
  rashers, cut into strips
700g (1½lb) white potatoes, cut
  into large chunks
200g can sweetcorn, drained
1kg (2¼lb) mussels, scrubbed,
  rinsed and beards removed (see
  Cook's Tip)
150ml (¼ pint) single cream
1 tbsp freshly chopped flat-leafed
  parsley
salt and ground black pepper

1 Melt the butter in a large pan, add the bacon and cook, stirring, until the strips separate. Add the potatoes and 150ml (¼ pint) water and season lightly with salt and pepper. Cover with a tight-fitting lid and cook for 10 minutes or until the potatoes are almost tender.

2 Add the sweetcorn and mussels to the pan, cover and bring to the boil, then reduce the heat and simmer for 2–3 minutes until the mussels open; discard any mussels that don't open. Add the cream and chopped parsley and serve immediately.

★ COOK'S TIP
To make sure mussels are safe to eat, check them carefully for cracks and split shells before cooking. Discard these, and any that do not close when tapped sharply. Any mussels that remain closed after cooking should also be thrown away.

Salmon and Bulgur Wheat Pilau

Preparation Time 5 minutes • Cooking Time 20 minutes • Serves 4 • Per Serving 323 calories, 11g fat (of which 2g saturates), 30g carbohydrate, 1.5g salt • Dairy Free • Easy

1 tbsp olive oil
1 onion, chopped
175g (6oz) bulgur wheat
450ml (¾ pint) vegetable stock
400g can pink salmon, drained and flaked
125g (4oz) spinach, roughly chopped
225g (8oz) frozen peas
zest and juice of 1 lemon
salt and ground black pepper

1 Heat the oil in a large pan, add the onion and cook until softened. Stir in the bulgur wheat to coat in the oil, then stir in the stock and bring to the boil. Cover, reduce the heat and simmer for 10–15 minutes until the stock has been fully absorbed.

2 Stir in the salmon, spinach, peas and lemon juice and cook until the spinach has wilted and the salmon and peas are heated through. Season to taste with salt and pepper and sprinkle with lemon zest before serving.

★ TRY SOMETHING DIFFERENT
Instead of salmon, use 200g (7oz) cooked peeled prawns and 200g (7oz) cherry tomatoes.

Salmon and Coconut Curry

Preparation Time 2 minutes • Cooking Time 18 minutes • Serves 4 • Per Serving 276 calories, 19g fat
(of which 3g saturates), 8g carbohydrate, 0.6g salt • Gluten Free • Dairy Free • Easy

1 tbsp olive oil
1 red onion, sliced
2 tbsp tikka masala curry paste
4 × 100g (3½oz) salmon steaks
400ml can coconut milk
juice of 1 lime
a handful of fresh coriander,
    roughly chopped

TO SERVE
lime wedges
boiled rice

1 Heat the oil in a pan. Add the onion and cook over a medium heat for 10 minutes until soft.

2 Add the curry paste to the pan and cook for 1 minute to warm the spices. Add the fish and cook for 2 minutes, turning it once to coat it in the spices.

3 Pour in the coconut milk and bring to the boil, then reduce the heat and simmer for 5 minutes or until the fish is cooked through.

4 Pour the lime juice over the fish and sprinkle with coriander. Serve with lime wedges to squeeze over the fish, and boiled rice to soak up the creamy sauce.

Cooking for Friends and Entertaining

Mixed Italian Bruschetta

Preparation Time 25 minutes • Serves 6 • Per Serving 398 calories, 15g fat (of which 7g saturates), 47g carbohydrate, 2.5g salt • Easy

1 long thin French stick
400g can butter beans, drained and rinsed
a small handful of fresh mint, shredded
zest and juice of ½ lemon
2 tbsp extra virgin olive oil, plus extra to drizzle
seeds from ½ pomegranate
150g (5oz) cherry tomatoes, quartered
200g (7oz) mozzarella bocconcini cheese, halved
1 tbsp fresh Pesto (see Cook's Tip, page 88)
2 tbsp fresh basil, chopped, plus

extra leaves to garnish
a small handful of rocket
6 slices bresaola
15g (½oz) freshly shaved Parmesan (see Cook's Tips, page 50)
75g (3oz) roasted red pepper, sliced
2 tbsp black olive tapenade (see Cook's Tips, page 80)
salt and ground black pepper

1 Cut the bread diagonally into 24 slices and toast in batches. Mash together the butter beans, mint, lemon zest and juice and oil. Season to taste with salt and pepper and stir in most of the pomegranate seeds. Set aside.

2 Put the tomatoes, mozzarella bocconcini, pesto and chopped basil into a separate bowl and stir to combine.

3 To assemble, spoon the bean mixture on to six toasts and garnish with the remaining pomegranate seeds. Top a further six with the mozzarella mixture and six with rocket, bresaola and Parmesan. Drizzle with the oil. For the final six bruschetta, put a few slices of roasted pepper on each toast. Add a little tapenade and garnish with a basil leaf.

Blinis with Easy Butter Bean and Sweet Pepper Hummus

Preparation Time 10 minutes • Serves 8 • Per Serving 160 calories, 8g fat (of which 1g saturates), 16g carbohydrate, 1.1g salt • Easy

400g can butter beans, drained and
   rinsed
300g tub reduced-fat hummus
10 whole Peppadew sweet peppers
   (see Cook's Tips, page 86)
a handful of flat-leafed parsley
128g pack ready-made blinis
finely grated lemon zest

1 Put the beans, hummus, sweet peppers and most of the parsley into a food processor and whiz to combine.

2 Spread the mixture on top of the blinis (you can freeze any leftover hummus: it will keep for up to a month). Top with a little lemon zest and more chopped parsley and serve.

Tangy Chicken Bites

Preparation Time 10 minutes • Makes 48 • Per Canapé 43 calories, 2g fat (of which 1g saturates), 4g carbohydrate, 0.1g salt • Easy

2 × 50g packs mini croustades
about 275g (10oz) fruity chutney, such as mango
2 roast chicken breasts, skinned, torn into small pieces
250g carton crème fraîche
a few fresh thyme sprigs

1 Place the croustades on a board. Spoon about ½ tsp chutney into each one. Top with a few shreds of chicken, a small dollop of crème fraîche and a few thyme leaves. Transfer the croustades to a large serving plate and serve immediately.

TRY SOMETHING DIFFERENT
● Use mini poppadoms instead of croustades.
● Replace the chutney with cranberry sauce.
● Instead of roast chicken, use turkey.

Chicken with Oyster Sauce

Preparation Time 10 minutes • Cooking Time about 18 minutes • Serves 4 • Per Serving 344 calories, 23g fat
(of which 3g saturates), 7g carbohydrate, 1.1g salt • Dairy Free • Easy

6 tbsp vegetable oil

450g (1lb) boneless, skinless
chicken breasts, cut into bite-size
pieces

3 tbsp oyster sauce

1 tbsp dark soy sauce

100ml (3½fl oz) chicken stock

2 tsp lemon juice

1 garlic clove, thinly sliced

6–8 large flat mushrooms, about
250g (9oz) total weight, sliced

125g (4oz) mangetouts

1 tsp cornflour mixed with 1 tbsp
water

1 tbsp toasted sesame oil

salt and ground black pepper

rice to serve

1 Heat 3 tbsp vegetable oil in a wok or large frying pan. Add the chicken and cook over a high heat, stirring continuously for 2–3 minutes until lightly browned. Remove the chicken with a slotted spoon and drain on kitchen paper.

2 Mix the oyster sauce with the soy sauce, stock and lemon juice. Add the chicken and mix thoroughly.

3 Heat the remaining vegetable oil in the pan over a high heat and stir-fry the garlic for about 30 seconds. Add the mushrooms and cook for

1 minute. Add the chicken mixture, cover and simmer for 8 minutes.

4 Stir in the mangetouts and cook for a further 2–3 minutes. Remove the pan from the heat and stir in the cornflour mixture. Put the pan back on the heat, add the sesame oil and stir until the sauce has thickened. Season with salt and pepper and serve immediately with rice.

Chicken with Wine and Capers

Preparation Time 5 minutes • Cooking Time 25 minutes • Serves 4 • Per Serving 234 calories, 10g fat (of which 5g saturates), trace carbohydrate, 0.3g salt • Gluten Free • Easy

1 tbsp olive oil
15g (½ oz) butter
4 small skinless chicken breasts
lemon wedges to garnish
boiled rice to serve

**FOR THE WINE AND CAPER
    SAUCE**
125ml (4fl oz) white wine
3 tbsp capers, rinsed and drained
juice of 1 lemon
15g (½oz) butter
1 tbsp freshly chopped flat-leafed
    parsley

1 Heat the oil and butter in a frying pan over a medium heat. Add the chicken breasts and fry for 10–12 minutes on each side until cooked through. Transfer to a warm plate, cover and keep warm.

2 To make the sauce, add the wine and capers to the same pan. Bring to the boil, then reduce the heat and simmer for 2–3 minutes until the wine is reduced by half. Add the lemon juice and butter and stir in the parsley.

3 Divide the chicken among four warmed plates, pour the sauce over the chicken, garnish each serving with a lemon wedge and serve immediately with boiled rice.

Basil and Lemon Chicken

Preparation Time 15 minutes, plus marinating • Serves 4 • Per Serving 331 calories, 25g fat (of which 5g saturates), 2g carbohydrate, 1.3g salt • Gluten Free • Dairy Free • Easy

grated zest of 1 lemon, plus 4 tbsp
    lemon juice
1 tsp caster sugar
1 tsp Dijon mustard
175ml (6fl oz) lemon-infused oil
4 tbsp freshly chopped basil
2 × 210g packs roast chicken
250g (9oz) baby leaf spinach
55g pack crisp bacon, broken into
    small pieces
salt and ground black pepper

1 Put the lemon zest and juice, sugar, mustard and oil into a small bowl and season with salt and pepper. Whisk together until thoroughly combined, then add the basil.

2 Remove any bones from the roast chicken, leave the skin attached and slice into four or eight pieces. Arrange the sliced chicken in a dish and pour the dressing over it, then cover and leave to marinate for at least 15 minutes.

3 Just before serving, lift the chicken from the dressing and put to one side.

4 Put the spinach into a large bowl, pour the dressing over it and toss together. Arrange the chicken on top of the spinach and sprinkle with the bacon. Serve immediately.

Spiced Chicken with Garlic Butter Beans

Preparation Time 10 minutes • Cooking Time 15 minutes • Serves 4 • Per Serving 443 calories, 16g fat (of which 3g saturates), 42g carbohydrate, 2g salt • Dairy Free • Easy

4 boneless, skinless chicken
    breasts, about 100g (3½oz) each
1 tbsp olive oil
1 tsp ground coriander
1 tsp ground cumin
100g (3½oz) couscous
3 tbsp extra virgin olive oil
1 garlic clove, sliced
2 × 400g cans butter beans, drained
    and rinsed
juice of 1 lemon
1 small red onion, thinly sliced
50g (2oz) marinated roasted
    peppers, drained
2 medium tomatoes, seeded and
    chopped
1 tbsp freshly chopped coriander
1 tbsp freshly chopped flat-leafed
    parsley
salt and ground black pepper
green salad and lemon wedges
    to serve

1 Put the chicken on a board, cover with clingfilm and flatten lightly with a rolling pin. Put the olive oil into a large bowl with the ground coriander and cumin. Mix together, then add the chicken and turn to coat.

2 Heat a large frying pan and cook the chicken for 5–7 minutes on each side until golden and the juices run clear when pierced with a sharp knife.

3 While the chicken is cooking, put the couscous into a bowl and add 100ml (3½fl oz) boiling water. Cover with clingfilm and set aside.

4 Put the extra virgin olive oil into a small pan with the garlic and butter beans and warm through for 3–4 minutes over a low heat. Stir in the lemon juice and season with salt and pepper.

5 Fluff up the couscous with a fork and tip in the warm butter beans. Add the onion, peppers, tomatoes and herbs and stir together. Slice each chicken breast into four pieces and arrange alongside the bean salad. Serve with a green salad and lemon wedges to squeeze over it.

Mediterranean Chicken

Preparation Time 5 minutes • Cooking Time 20 minutes • Serves 4 • Per Serving 223 calories, 7g fat
(of which 1g saturates), 3g carbohydrate, 0.2g salt • Gluten Free • Dairy Free • Easy

1 red pepper, seeded and chopped
2 tbsp capers
2 tbsp freshly chopped rosemary
2 tbsp olive oil
4 skinless chicken breasts, about
    125g (4oz) each
salt and ground black pepper
rice or new potatoes to serve

1 Preheat the oven to 200°C (180°C
fan oven) mark 6. Put the red
pepper into a bowl with the capers,
rosemary and oil. Season with salt
and pepper and mix well.

2 Put the chicken breasts into an
ovenproof dish and spoon the
pepper mixture over the top. Roast
for 15–20 minutes until the chicken
is cooked through and the topping
is hot. Serve with rice or new
potatoes.

★ TRY SOMETHING
DIFFERENT
*Use chopped black olives instead of
the capers.*

Garlic and Thyme Chicken

Preparation Time 10 minutes • Cooking Time 10–15 minutes • Serves 4 • Per Serving 135 calories, 6g fat (of which 1g saturates), trace carbohydrate, 0.2g salt • Gluten Free • Dairy Free • Easy

2 garlic cloves, crushed
2 tbsp freshly chopped thyme
  leaves
2 tbsp olive oil
4 chicken thighs
salt and ground black pepper

1 Preheat the barbecue or grill. Mix the garlic with the thyme and oil in a large bowl. Season with salt and pepper.

2 Using a sharp knife, make two or three slits in each chicken thigh. Put the chicken into the bowl and toss to coat thoroughly. Barbecue or grill for 5–7 minutes on each side until golden and cooked through.

Moroccan Spiced Chicken Kebabs

Preparation Time 10 minutes, plus marinating • Cooking Time 10–12 minutes • Serves 4 • Per Serving 190 calories, 7g fat (of which 1g saturates), 1g carbohydrate, 0.2g salt • Gluten Free • Dairy Free • Easy

2 tbsp olive oil
15g (½oz) flat-leafed parsley
1 garlic clove
½ tsp paprika
1 tsp ground cumin
zest and juice of 1 lemon
4 skinless chicken breasts, cut into
**   bite-size chunks**
salt
shredded lettuce, sliced cucumber
**   and tomatoes, and lime wedges**
**   to serve**

1 Put the oil into a blender and add the parsley, garlic, paprika, cumin, lemon zest and juice and a pinch of salt. Whiz to make a paste.

2 Put the chicken into a medium-sized shallow dish and rub in the spice paste. Leave to marinate for at least 20 minutes. Preheat the grill to high. Soak some wooden skewers in water.

3 Thread the marinated chicken on to the skewers and grill for 10–12 minutes, turning every now and then, until the meat is cooked

through. Serve with shredded lettuce, sliced cucumber and tomatoes, and lime wedges.

⭐ TRY SOMETHING DIFFERENT
Instead of chicken, use 700g (1½lb) lean lamb fillet or leg of lamb, cut into chunks.

Pork Steaks with Sage and Parma Ham

Preparation Time 5 minutes • Cooking Time 10 minutes • Serves 4 • Per Serving 328 calories, 20g fat, (of which 9g saturates), 4g carbohydrate, 0.8g salt • Gluten Free • Easy

4 pork shoulder steaks, about 150g (5oz) each
4 thin slices Parma ham or pancetta
6 sage leaves
1 tbsp oil
150ml (¼ pint) pure unsweetened apple juice
50g (2oz) chilled butter, diced
squeeze of lemon juice
ground black pepper
steamed cabbage or kale and mashed sweet potatoes to serve

1 Put the pork steaks on a board. Lay a slice of Parma ham or pancetta and a sage leaf on each pork steak, then secure to the meat with a wooden cocktail stick. Season with pepper.

2 Heat the oil in a large heavy-based frying pan and fry the pork for 3–4 minutes on each side until golden brown.

3 Pour the apple juice into the pan, stirring and scraping up the sediment from the base of the pan. Let the liquid bubble until reduced by half. Lift the pork out on to a warmed plate.

4 Return the pan to the heat, add the butter and swirl until melted into the pan juices. Add lemon juice to taste, then pour the sauce over the pork. Serve with cabbage or curly kale and sweet potatoes.

Pork with Artichokes and Beans

Preparation Time 10 minutes • Cooking Time 8 minutes • Serves 4 • Per Serving 473 calories, 36g fat (of which 6g saturates), 17g carbohydrate, 3.7g salt • Gluten Free • Dairy Free • Easy

2 tbsp vegetable oil

2 pork fillets, about 275g (10oz)
   each, cut into 1cm (½in) slices

2 tbsp freshly chopped thyme
   leaves

8 tbsp olive oil

400g can artichoke hearts, drained,
   rinsed and quartered

400g can flageolet beans, drained
   and rinsed

185g jar pitted green olives, drained
   and rinsed

juice of 1 lemon

salt and ground black pepper

1 Heat the vegetable oil in a frying pan over a medium heat and fry the pork for 2 minutes on each side. Add the thyme and season with salt and pepper.

2 Meanwhile, heat the olive oil in a separate pan over a medium heat. Add the artichokes and beans and cook for 3–4 minutes. Add the olives and lemon juice and season with pepper.

3 Put the pork on top of the artichokes, beans and olives and serve immediately.

Spiced Pork with Lemon Pasta

Preparation Time 10 minutes · Cooking Time 12 minutes · Serves 6 · Per Serving 733 calories, 44g fat (of which 28g saturates), 71g carbohydrate, 1.8g salt · Easy

8 thick pork sausages

500g (1lb 2oz) pasta shells or other shapes

100ml (3½fl oz) chicken stock

grated zest of 1 lemon

juice of ½ lemon

a large pinch of dried chilli flakes

300ml (½ pint) half-fat crème fraîche

2 tbsp freshly chopped flat-leafed parsley

salt and ground black pepper

25g (1oz) freshly grated Parmesan to serve

1 Remove the skin from the sausages and pinch the meat into small pieces. Heat a non-stick frying pan over a medium heat. When hot, add the sausagemeat and cook for 5 minutes, stirring occasionally, or until cooked through and browned.

2 Meanwhile, cook the pasta in a large pan of lightly salted boiling water according to the pack instructions until al dente.

3 Add the stock to the sausagemeat, bring to the boil and let bubble, stirring, for 2–3 minutes

until the liquid has reduced right down. Add the lemon zest and juice, chilli flakes and crème fraîche. Season well with salt and pepper. Continue to cook for 3–4 minutes until reduced and thickened slightly.

4 Drain the pasta and return to the pan. Stir the parsley into the sauce and toss with the pasta. Serve immediately, with grated Parmesan.

Fennel Pork with Cabbage and Apple

Preparation Time 10 minutes • Cooking Time 6–10 minutes • Serves 4 • Per Serving 276 calories, 12g fat
(of which 3g saturates), 9g carbohydrate, 0.3g salt • Gluten Free • Dairy Free • Easy

2 tbsp olive oil
½ tbsp fennel seeds, crushed
1 tbsp freshly chopped sage
4 lean pork medallions, 125g (4oz)
   each
½ small red cabbage, shredded
450g (1lb) purple sprouting
   broccoli, tough ends removed
1 apple, cored and sliced into rings
salt and ground black pepper

1 Put 1 tbsp oil into a large shallow bowl. Add the fennel seeds and sage, season with salt and pepper and mix well. Add the pork and rub the mixture into the meat.

2 Heat the remaining oil in a wok or large frying pan and stir-fry the cabbage and broccoli for 6–8 minutes until starting to char.

3 Meanwhile, heat a non-stick griddle until hot and fry the pork for 2–3 minutes on each side until cooked through. Remove and set aside. Add the apple rings to the pan and griddle for 1–2 minutes on each side until starting to char and caramelise. Serve with the pork and vegetables.

Lamb with Orange and Mint

Preparation Time 10 minutes • Cooking Time 20 minutes • Serves 4 • Per Serving 451 calories, 32g fat (of which 11g saturates), 6g carbohydrate, 1.1g salt • Gluten Free • Dairy Free • Easy

4 tbsp olive oil

4 lamb steaks, about 700g (1½lb) total weight

185g jar chargrilled sweet red peppers, drained and roughly chopped

50g (2oz) black olives

1 orange

juice of 1 lemon

1 small bunch of mint, roughly chopped

salt and ground black pepper

1 Heat 2 tbsp oil in a large non-stick frying pan. Brown the lamb in the hot oil, turning occasionally, until the meat has formed a deep golden-brown crust all over.

2 Reduce the heat and add the peppers and olives to the pan. Chop up the orange, squeeze the juice directly into the pan and add the orange pieces for extra flavour. Add the lemon juice and the remaining oil.

3 Simmer for 5 minutes, stirring to break down the peppers a little. Stir the mint into the pan. Season to taste with salt and pepper and serve.

★ TRY SOMETHING DIFFERENT

Add a handful of shredded spinach with the mint.

Lamb with Spicy Couscous

Preparation Time 10 minutes • Cooking Time 15 minutes • Serves 4 • Per Serving 675 calories, 37g fat (of which 13g saturates), 44g carbohydrate, 0.5g salt • Easy

2 lamb fillets, about 400g (14oz) each
5 tbsp olive oil
1 aubergine, cut into 1cm (½in) dice
1 tsp ground cumin
½ tsp ground cinnamon
225g (8oz) quick-cook couscous
1 large fresh red chilli, seeded and finely chopped (see Cook's Tips, page 42)
3 tbsp freshly chopped mint
75g (3oz) raisins, soaked in hot water and drained
salt and ground black pepper
Greek yogurt to serve

1 Trim the lamb fillets, rub in 1 tbsp oil and season well with salt and pepper. Heat a heavy-based non-stick pan, add the lamb and fry for 15 minutes, turning regularly. Remove from the pan and leave to rest for 5 minutes (see Cook's Tip).

2 Meanwhile, toss the aubergine in the cumin and cinnamon, then fry in 2 tbsp oil for 10 minutes or until softened. Prepare the couscous according to the pack instructions, then fluff the grains using a fork. Add the aubergine, chilli, 2 tbsp mint, the raisins and the remaining oil to the couscous. Season well with salt and pepper.

3 To serve, slice the lamb and place on top of the couscous. Drizzle with Greek yogurt, sprinkle with the remaining chopped mint and serve immediately.

⭐ COOK'S TIP
Leaving the lamb to rest for 5 minutes allows the juices to set and they won't run out.

Lamb with Tapenade

Preparation Time 5 minutes, plus marinating • Cooking Time 8–10 minutes • Serves 4 • Per Serving 579 calories, 34g fat (of which 15g saturates), 0g carbohydrate, 0.4g salt • Gluten Free • Dairy Free • Easy

6 tbsp olive oil

4 tbsp tapenade (see Cook's Tips, page 80)

2 tbsp Pernod or Ricard

2 garlic cloves, crushed

8 loin lamb chops, about 125g (4oz) each

ground black pepper

TO SERVE

grilled sliced fennel and courgettes

4 lemon halves

1 Mix the oil with the tapenade, Pernod or Ricard and the garlic, then rub into the lamb chops and season with black pepper. Leave to marinate for at least 30 minutes or overnight.

2 Preheat the barbecue or griddle. Cook the chops for 4–5 minutes on each side. Serve with lightly grilled fennel and courgette slices, and lemon halves to squeeze over them.

★ COOK'S TIP

The marinade is ideal for other cuts of lamb, such as steaks or fillets, or spread it over a boned shoulder or leg.

Steak with Onions and Tagliatelle

Preparation Time 10 minutes • Cooking Time 20 minutes • Serves 4 • Per Serving 557 calories, 26g fat (of which 16g saturates), 51g carbohydrate, 0.2g salt • Easy

225g (8oz) tagliatelle
2 × 200g (7oz) sirloin steaks
2 red onions, thinly sliced
200g (7oz) low-fat crème fraîche
2 tbsp freshly chopped flat-leafed parsley
salt and ground black pepper

1 Cook the pasta in a large pan of boiling water according to the pack instructions; do not overcook – it should be al dente. Drain well.

2 Meanwhile, season the steaks on both sides with salt and pepper. Heat a non-stick frying pan until really hot and fry the steaks for 2–3 minutes on each side until brown but still pink inside. Remove from the pan and set aside.

3 Add the onions to the pan and stir-fry for 8–10 minutes until softened and golden. Add a little water if they're sticking. Season, reduce the heat and stir in the crème fraîche.

4 Cut the fat off the steaks and discard, then cut the meat into thin strips. Add to the pan and cook briskly for 1–2 minutes, then stir in the pasta. Add the parsley, toss again and serve immediately.

Szechuan Beef

Preparation Time 15 minutes, plus marinating • Cooking Time 5–10 minutes • Serves 4 • Per Serving 298 calories, 14g fat (of which 4g saturates), 15g carbohydrate, 0.6g salt • Dairy Free • Easy

350g (12oz) beef skirt or rump
    steak, cut into thin strips
5 tbsp hoisin sauce
4 tbsp dry sherry
2 tbsp vegetable oil
2 red or green chillies, seeded and
    finely chopped (see Cook's Tips,
    page 42)
1 large onion, thinly sliced
2 garlic cloves, crushed
2 red peppers, seeded and cut into
    diamond shapes
2.5cm (1in) piece fresh root ginger,
    peeled and grated
225g can bamboo shoots, drained
    and sliced
1 tbsp sesame oil

1 Put the beef into a bowl, add the hoisin sauce and sherry and stir to coat. Cover and leave to marinate for 30 minutes.

2 Heat the vegetable oil in a wok or large frying pan until smoking hot. Add the chillies, onion and garlic and stir-fry over a medium heat for 3–4 minutes until softened. Remove with a slotted spoon and set aside. Add the red peppers, increase the heat and stir-fry for a few seconds. Remove and set aside.

3 Add the steak and marinade to the pan in batches. Stir-fry each batch over a high heat for about 1 minute, then remove with a slotted spoon.

4 Return the vegetables to the pan. Add the ginger and bamboo shoots, then the beef, and stir-fry for a further 1 minute or until heated through. Transfer to a warmed serving dish, sprinkle the sesame oil over the top and serve immediately.

Sesame Beef

Preparation Time 10 minutes • Cooking Time 10 minutes • Serves 4 • Per Serving 207 calories, 10g fat (of which 3g saturates), 4g carbohydrate, 2g salt • Dairy Free • Easy

2 tbsp soy sauce
2 tbsp Worcestershire sauce
2 tsp tomato purée
juice of ½ lemon
1 tbsp sesame seeds
1 garlic clove, crushed
400g (14oz) rump steak, sliced
1 tbsp vegetable oil
3 small pak choi, chopped
1 bunch of spring onions, sliced
freshly cooked egg noodles or
    tagliatelle to serve

1 Put the soy sauce and Worcestershire sauce, tomato purée, lemon juice, sesame seeds and garlic into a bowl. Add the steak and toss to coat.

2 Heat the oil in a large wok or non-stick frying pan until hot. Add the steak and sear well. Remove from the wok and set aside.

3 Add any sauce from the bowl to the wok and heat for 1 minute. Add the pak choi, spring onions and steak and stir-fry for 5 minutes. Add freshly cooked and drained noodles, toss and serve immediately.

★ TRY SOMETHING DIFFERENT
Use 400g (14oz) pork escalope cut into strips instead of beef. Cook for 5 minutes before removing from the pan at step 2.

Teriyaki Beef Stir-fry

Preparation Time 20 minutes, plus marinating • Cooking Time 5 minutes • Serves 4 • Per Serving 275 calories, 16g fat (of which 5g saturates), 6g carbohydrate, 2g salt • Gluten Free • Dairy Free • Easy

450g (1lb) beef fillet, sliced as thinly as possible, then cut into strips 1cm (½in) wide
2 tbsp vegetable or groundnut oil
225g (8oz) carrots, cut into matchsticks
½ cucumber, halved lengthways, seeded and cut into matchsticks
4–6 spring onions, thinly sliced diagonally
noodles tossed in a little sesame oil and wasabi paste (optional, see Cook's Tip) to serve

FOR THE TERIYAKI MARINADE
4 tbsp tamari (wheat-free Japanese soy sauce)
4 tbsp mirin or medium sherry
1 garlic clove, finely chopped
2.5cm (1in) piece fresh root ginger, peeled and finely chopped

1 Put all the ingredients for the marinade into a shallow bowl and mix well. Add the beef and turn to coat. Cover, chill and leave to marinate for at least 30 minutes, preferably overnight.

2 Drain the beef, reserving any marinade. Heat a wok or large frying pan, then add the oil and heat until it is smoking. Add the carrots, cucumber and spring onions and fry over a high heat for 2 minutes or until the edges are well browned. Remove from the pan and set aside.

3 Add the beef to the pan and stir-fry over a very high heat for 2 minutes.

4 Return the vegetables to the pan and add the reserved marinade. Stir-fry for 1–2 minutes until heated through. Serve immediately with noodles tossed in a little sesame oil and a small amount of wasabi paste, if you like.

★ COOK'S TIP
Wasabi paste is a Japanese condiment, green in colour and extremely hot – a little goes a long way. It is available from some supermarkets.

Beef Stroganoff

Preparation Time 10 minutes • Cooking Time about 20 minutes • Serves 4 • Per Serving 750 calories, 60g fat (of which 35g saturates), 3g carbohydrate, 0.5g salt • Gluten Free • Easy

700g (1½lb) rump or fillet steak, trimmed
50g (2oz) unsalted butter or 4 tbsp olive oil
1 onion, thinly sliced
225g (8oz) brown-cap mushrooms, sliced
3 tbsp brandy
1 tsp French mustard
200ml (7fl oz) crème fraîche
100ml (3½fl oz) double cream
3 tbsp freshly chopped flat-leafed parsley
salt and ground black pepper
rice or noodles to serve

1 Cut the steak into strips about 5mm (¼in) wide and 5cm (2in) long.

2 Heat half the butter or oil in a large heavy frying pan over a medium heat. Add the onion and cook gently for 10 minutes or until soft and golden. Remove with a slotted spoon and put to one side. Add the mushrooms to the pan and cook, stirring, for 2–3 minutes until golden brown; remove and put to one side.

3 Increase the heat and add the remaining butter or oil to the pan.

Quickly fry the meat, in two or three batches, for 2–3 minutes, stirring constantly to ensure even browning. Remove from the pan. Add the brandy to the pan and allow it to bubble to reduce.

4 Put all the meat, onion and mushrooms back in the pan. Reduce the heat and stir in the mustard, crème fraîche and cream. Heat through, stir in most of the parsley and season with salt and pepper. Serve with rice or noodles, with the remaining parsley scattered over the top.

Oven-poached Cod with Herbs

Preparation Time 10 minutes • Cooking Time 10 minutes • Serves 4 • Per Serving 170 calories, 2g fat (of which trace saturates), 1g carbohydrate, 0.5g salt • Gluten Free • Dairy Free • Easy

10 spring onions, sliced
2 garlic cloves, crushed
6 tbsp shredded fresh mint
6 tbsp freshly chopped flat-leafed
    parsley
juice of ½ lemon
150ml (¼ pint) fish, chicken or
    vegetable stock
4 cod fillets, about 200g (7oz) each
salt and ground black pepper
lemon wedges to garnish
mashed potatoes to serve

1 Preheat the oven to 230°C (210°C fan oven) mark 8. Combine the spring onions (putting some of the green part to one side), garlic, mint, parsley, lemon juice and stock in an ovenproof dish that can hold the cod in a single layer.

2 Put the cod on the herb and garlic mixture and turn to moisten. Season with salt and pepper, then roast for 8–10 minutes.

3 Sprinkle with the reserved spring onion, garnish with lemon wedges and serve with mashed potatoes.

★ TRY SOMETHING DIFFERENT
There are lots of alternatives to cod: try sea bass, gurnard or pollack.

Roasted Cod with Fennel

Preparation Time 3 minutes • Cooking Time 20 minutes • Serves 4 • Per Serving 306 calories, 14g fat
(of which 7g saturates), 9g carbohydrate, 0.4g salt • Gluten Free • Dairy Free • Easy

50g (2oz) butter
1 tbsp olive oil
2 red onions, finely sliced
2 small or 1 large fennel bulb, finely
 sliced
2 tbsp chopped dill, plus extra
 to garnish
150ml (¼ pint) dry white wine
4 × 150g (5oz) pieces cod
salt and ground black pepper
new potatoes and green beans
 to serve

1 Preheat the oven to 200°C (180°C fan oven) mark 6. Heat the butter and oil in a flameproof casserole dish over a medium heat. When sizzling, add the onions and fennel, then cover and cook, stirring occasionally, for 7 minutes or until soft and translucent.

2 Add the dill and wine and bring quickly to the boil. Put the fish on top of the fennel mixture and season with salt and pepper. Put the casserole dish into the oven and cook for 10 minutes, basting the fish occasionally with the juices.

3 Sprinkle with plenty of extra dill and serve immediately with new potatoes and green beans.

⭐ TRY SOMETHING DIFFERENT
● *Use haddock, coley or whiting instead of the cod.*
● *Stir 1 tbsp capers in with the dill and wine.*

Poached Thai Salmon

Preparation Time 10 minutes • Cooking Time 15 minutes • Serves 4 • Per Serving 484 calories, 19g fat (of which 3g saturates), 42g carbohydrate, 1.8g salt • Gluten Free • Dairy Free • Easy

200g (7oz) Thai jasmine rice
1 tbsp sesame oil
1 red chilli, seeded and finely chopped (see Cook's Tips, page 42)
5cm (2in) piece fresh root ginger, peeled and finely chopped
1 garlic clove, crushed
1–2 tbsp miso paste (see Cook's Tips)
2 tsp Thai fish sauce (see Cook's Tips)
4 skinless salmon fillets, about 150g (5oz) each
150g (5oz) fresh shiitake mushrooms, sliced

250g (9oz) pak choi, roughly chopped
100g (3½oz) baby leaf spinach
1 lime, quartered

1 Put the rice into a small pan with 400ml (14fl oz) boiling water. Cover and bring to the boil, then reduce the heat to low and cook according to the pack instructions.

2 Heat the oil in a large shallow pan or wok, add the chilli, ginger and garlic and cook for 1–2 minutes. Add the miso paste and fish sauce, then pour in 500ml (18fl oz) hot water. Add the salmon and mushrooms, then cover and simmer for 7–8 minutes until fish is just cooked.

3 Steam the pak choi and spinach over boiling water for 4–5 minutes. Serve the salmon with the sauce, rice and vegetables, and lime wedges to squeeze over it.

★ COOK'S TIPS
● Miso (fermented barley and soya beans) contains beneficial live enzymes that can be destroyed by boiling. Miso is best added as a flavouring at the end of cooking. It's available from Asian shops, health-food shops and larger supermarkets.
● Thai fish sauce is widely used in Southeast Asian cooking and is made from fermented anchovies. It adds a salty flavour to food and is called 'nam pla' in Thailand.

Mediterranean Salmon

Preparation Time 15 minutes, plus marinating • Cooking Time 10–12 minutes • Serves 12 • Per Serving 251 calories, 18g fat (of which 3g saturates), 1g carbohydrate, 0.8g salt • Gluten Free • Easy

12 × 125g (4oz) salmon fillets, skinned
5 tbsp ready-made pesto
50g (2oz) sun-dried tomatoes, chopped
100g (3½oz) black olives
3 lemons
new potatoes and a green salad to serve

1 Mix the salmon, pesto, tomatoes and olives in a large bowl. Sprinkle with the zest of 1 lemon, then cover and chill for 30 minutes.

2 Preheat the oven to 200°C (180°C fan oven) mark 6. Arrange the salmon in a large ovenproof serving dish and spoon the tomato, olive and pesto marinade over it.

3 Cut each of the remaining lemons into six wedges and put around the salmon. Cook for 10–12 minutes until the fish flakes when pushed with a knife, then serve with new potatoes and salad.

★ GET AHEAD
To prepare ahead *Complete the recipe to the end of step 1, then cover and chill for up to two days.*
To use *Complete the recipe.*

Salmon Laksa Curry

Preparation Time 10 minutes • Cooking Time about 20 minutes • Serves 4 • Per Serving 570 calories, 22g fat (of which 3g saturates), 55g carbohydrate, 1.9g salt • Gluten Free • Dairy Free • Easy

1 tbsp olive oil
1 onion, thinly sliced
3 tbsp laksa paste (see Cook's Tip)
200ml (7fl oz) coconut milk
900ml (1½ pints) hot vegetable stock
200g (7oz) baby sweetcorn, halved lengthways
600g (1lb 5oz) piece skinless salmon fillet, cut into 1cm (½in) slices
225g (8oz) baby leaf spinach
250g (9oz) medium rice noodles
salt and ground black pepper

TO GARNISH
2 spring onions, sliced diagonally
2 tbsp freshly chopped coriander
1 lime, cut into wedges

1 Heat the oil in a wok or large frying pan, then add the onion and fry over a medium heat for 10 minutes, stirring, until golden. Add the laksa paste and cook for 2 minutes.

2 Add the coconut milk, hot stock and sweetcorn and season with salt and pepper. Bring to the boil, then reduce the heat and simmer for 5 minutes.

3 Add the salmon slices and spinach, stirring to immerse them in the liquid. Cook for 4 minutes or until the fish is opaque all the way through.

4 Meanwhile, put the noodles into a large heatproof bowl, pour boiling water over to cover and soak for 30 seconds. Drain well, then stir them into the curry. Pour the curry into four warmed bowls and garnish with the spring onions and coriander. Serve immediately with lime wedges.

⭐ COOK'S TIP
Laksa paste is a hot and spicy paste; you could use Thai curry paste instead.

⭐ TRY SOMETHING DIFFERENT
Instead of the medium rice noodles try using rice vermicelli, or leave out the noodles and serve with basmati rice.

Kerala Fish Curry

Preparation Time 10 minutes • Cooking Time about 20 minutes • Serves 4 • Per Serving 189 calories, 9g fat (of which 1g saturates), 5g carbohydrate, 0.5g salt • Gluten Free • Dairy Free • A Little Effort

4 skinless sole or plaice fillets, about 125g (4oz) each
2 tbsp light olive oil
1 onion, thinly sliced
1 large garlic clove, crushed
1 green chilli, slit lengthways, seeds in (see Cook's Tips, page 42)
2.5cm (1in) piece fresh root ginger, peeled and grated
1 tsp ground turmeric
1 tbsp garam masala, or about 12 curry leaves (see Cook's Tips)
200ml (7fl oz) coconut milk
1 tbsp freshly squeezed lime juice, white wine vinegar or tamarind paste (see Cook's Tips)
salt and ground black pepper

TO SERVE
basmati rice
fresh banana leaves (optional, see Cook's Tip)
1 lime, cut into wedges

1 Roll up the fish fillets from head to tail and put to one side.

2 Heat the oil in a deep frying pan over a medium heat. Stir in the onion, garlic, chilli and ginger and stir-fry for 5–7 minutes until the onion is soft. Add the turmeric and garam masala (or curry leaves, if using) and fry for a further 1–2 minutes until aromatic.

3 Pour the coconut milk into the pan along with 200ml (7fl oz) water and bring to the boil. Reduce the heat and simmer very gently, uncovered, for 7–10 minutes until slightly thickened. The sauce should be the consistency of single cream. Stir in the lime juice, vinegar or tamarind. Check the seasoning and adjust if necessary.

4 When you're ready to serve, carefully lower the rolls of fish into the hot sauce to prevent splashing and simmer very gently for 1–2 minutes until just cooked. Serve on a bed of basmati rice, in deep bowls lined with strips of banana leaves if you like, with a wedge of lime to squeeze over it.

⭐ GET AHEAD
To prepare ahead Make the sauce up to 4 hours ahead.
To use Gently reheat to simmering point before you add the fish.

⭐ COOK'S TIPS
● Buy curry leaves and banana leaves from Asian shops.
● Tamarind paste has a very sharp, sour flavour and is widely used in Asian and Southeast Asian cooking.

Salmon with a Spicy Yogurt Crust

Preparation Time 10 minutes • Cooking Time 10 minutes • Serves 4 • Per Serving 250 calories, 14g fat (of which 3g saturates), 3g carbohydrate, 0.2g salt • Gluten Free • Easy

3 tbsp freshly chopped coriander
1 garlic clove, crushed
2.5cm (1in) piece fresh root ginger, peeled and grated
½ tsp each ground cumin and coriander
¼ tsp cayenne pepper
150g (5oz) natural yogurt
4 × 125g (4oz) salmon fillets
salt
lime wedges and herb salad to serve

1 Preheat the grill. Mix together the chopped coriander, garlic, ginger, ground cumin and coriander, the cayenne, yogurt and a pinch of salt. Add the salmon and turn to coat.

2 Grill the fish for 7–10 minutes or until cooked through. Serve with lime wedges to squeeze over the fish and a herb salad.

★ TRY SOMETHING DIFFERENT
Use another fish instead of salmon: try trout or plump mackerel fillets.

Warm Spiced Salmon Niçoise

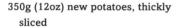

Preparation Time 15 minutes • Cooking Time 15 minutes • Serves 4 • Per Serving 480 calories, 28g fat (of which 6g saturates), 18g carbohydrate, 0.6g salt • Gluten Free • Easy

350g (12oz) new potatoes, thickly sliced

175g (6oz) fine green beans, halved

175g (6oz) cherry tomatoes, halved

1 small red onion, cut into thin wedges

4 × 150–175g (5–6oz) salmon fillets, skinned

15g (½oz) butter, melted

1 tbsp coriander seeds, crushed

½ tsp dried crushed chillies

4 tbsp Caesar Dressing (see Cook's Tip)

flaked sea salt and ground black pepper

fresh chives to garnish

1 Cook the potatoes in lightly salted boiling water for 8–10 minutes until just tender, adding the beans for the last 2 minutes. Drain well, then transfer to a bowl with the tomatoes and onion wedges. Meanwhile, preheat the grill.

2 Cut each salmon fillet into three strips. Place the strips in four piles on a baking sheet and brush each pile with the melted butter. Mix the crushed coriander seeds with the chillies and a little sea salt and sprinkle evenly over the salmon. Place under the hot grill for 4–5 minutes until just cooked through.

3 Add 1 tbsp water to the dressing to thin it slightly (it should be the consistency of single cream). Spoon three-quarters of the dressing over the vegetables and toss to coat. Season well.

4 Divide the vegetables among four plates, top with the salmon and drizzle the remaining dressing around the edge of the salad. Garnish with chives and serve.

★ COOK'S TIP

Caesar Dressing
Put 1 egg, 1 garlic clove, juice of
½ lemon, 2 tsp Dijon mustard and
1 tsp balsamic vinegar into a food
processor and whiz until smooth, then,
with the motor running, gradually add
150ml (¼ pint) sunflower oil and whiz
until smooth. Season with salt and
pepper, cover and chill. It will keep
for up to three days.

Scallops with Ginger

Preparation Time 15 minutes • Cooking Time 3 minutes • Serves 4 • Per Serving 197 calories, 7g fat (of which 1g saturates), 6g carbohydrate, 2g salt • Dairy Free • Easy

2 tbsp vegetable oil

500g (1lb 2oz) shelled large scallops, cut into 5mm (¼in) slices

4 celery sticks, sliced diagonally

1 bunch of spring onions, sliced diagonally

25g (1oz) piece fresh root ginger, peeled and shredded

2 large garlic cloves, sliced

¼ tsp chilli powder

2 tbsp lemon juice

2 tbsp light soy sauce

3 tbsp freshly chopped coriander

salt and ground black pepper

rice to serve

1 Heat the oil in a wok or large frying pan. Add the scallops, celery, spring onions, ginger, garlic and chilli powder and stir-fry over a high heat for 2 minutes or until the vegetables are just tender.

2 Pour in the lemon juice and soy sauce, allow to bubble up, then stir in about 2 tbsp chopped coriander and season with salt and pepper. Sprinkle with the remaining coriander and serve with rice.

Peppered Tuna with Olive and Herb Salsa

Preparation Time 15 minutes • Cooking Time 8–12 minutes • Serves 4 • Per Serving 398 calories, 32g fat (of which 12g saturates), 1g carbohydrate, 1.9g salt • Gluten Free • Dairy Free • Easy

1 tsp olive oil

zest and juice of 1 lime, plus lime wedges to serve

1 tbsp cracked mixed peppercorns

4 × 150g (5oz) tuna steaks

grilled tomatoes to serve

FOR THE OLIVE AND HERB SALSA

1 tbsp extra virgin olive oil

1 tbsp each pitted black and green olives, roughly chopped

zest and juice of ½ lemon

2 tbsp freshly chopped parsley

1 tbsp freshly chopped coriander

1 tbsp capers, roughly chopped

salt and ground black pepper

1 Put the olive oil into a large shallow bowl, add the lime zest and juice and peppercorns and stir to mix. Add the tuna and turn to coat in the oil.

2 Heat a non-stick griddle pan until hot. Cook the tuna steaks, two at a time, for 2–3 minutes on each side.

3 Meanwhile, put all the ingredients for the salsa into a bowl and stir to combine. Season to taste and mix well. Serve the tuna with the salsa and grilled tomatoes, and lime wedges to squeeze over it.

★ TRY SOMETHING DIFFERENT

Use swordfish instead of tuna.

Plaice with Herb and Polenta Crust

Preparation Time 15 minutes • Cooking Time 4–6 minutes • Serves 2 • Per Serving 376 calories, 17g fat (of which 3g saturates), 19g carbohydrate, 0.6g salt • Gluten Free • Dairy Free • Easy

1 tsp finely chopped rosemary or
   1 tsp finely snipped chives
1 tsp finely chopped thyme
2 garlic cloves, very finely chopped
50g (2oz) polenta
finely grated zest and juice of
   2 small lemons
2 plaice fillets, about 175g (6oz)
   each, skinned
1 large egg
2 tbsp olive oil
salt and ground black pepper
roasted tomatoes, green beans and
   lemon wedges to serve

1 Combine the herbs, garlic and polenta on a flat plate. Add the lemon zest, salt and pepper and mix well. Wipe the plaice fillets with kitchen paper.

2 Beat the egg in a shallow dish, dip the fish fillets into the egg and coat them with the polenta mixture, pressing it on well.

3 Heat the oil in a very large frying pan over a high heat. When hot, add the fish, turn the heat down to medium and cook for 2–3 minutes on each side, depending on the thickness of the fillets. Drain on kitchen paper. Serve with lemon juice poured over them, with roasted tomatoes, green beans and extra lemon wedges.

Saffron Paella

Preparation Time 5 minutes • Cooking Time 20 minutes • Serves 6 • Per Serving 609 calories, 22g fat (of which 6g saturates), 59g carbohydrate, 1.5g salt • Dairy Free • Easy

½ tsp saffron threads
900ml–1.1 litres (1½–2 pints) hot chicken stock
5 tbsp olive oil
2 × 70g packs sliced chorizo sausage
6 boneless, skinless chicken thighs, each cut into three pieces
1 large onion, chopped
4 large garlic cloves, crushed
1 tsp paprika
2 red peppers, seeded and sliced
400g can chopped tomatoes in tomato juice
350g (12oz) long-grain rice
200ml (7fl oz) dry sherry
500g pack ready-cooked mussels
200g (7oz) cooked tiger prawns, drained
juice of ½ lemon
salt and ground black pepper
fresh flat-leafed parsley sprigs to garnish (optional)
lemon wedges to serve

1 Add the saffron to the hot stock and leave to infuse for 30 minutes. Meanwhile, heat half the oil in a large heavy-based frying pan. Add half the chorizo and fry for 3–4 minutes until crisp. Remove with a slotted spoon and drain on kitchen paper. Repeat with the remaining chorizo, then put to one side.

2 Heat 1 tbsp oil in the pan, add half the chicken and cook for 3–5 minutes until pale golden brown. Remove from the pan and put to one side. Cook the remaining chicken and put to one side.

3 Reduce the heat slightly, heat the remaining oil and add the onion. Cook for 5 minutes or until soft. Add the garlic and paprika and cook for 1 minute. Put the chicken back into the pan, then add the peppers and the tomatoes.

4 Stir the rice into the pan, then add one-third of the stock and bring to the boil. Season with salt and pepper, reduce the heat and simmer, uncovered, stirring continuously until most of the liquid has been absorbed.

5 Add the remaining stock, a little at a time, allowing the liquid to become absorbed after each addition (this should take about 25 minutes). Add the sherry and cook for a further 2 minutes.

6 Add the mussels and their juices to the pan with the prawns, lemon juice and reserved chorizo. Cook for 5 minutes to heat through. Adjust the seasoning and garnish with the parsley, if you like, and serve with lemon wedges.

Tuna with Coriander Rice

Preparation Time 10 minutes • Cooking Time about 5 minutes • Serves 4 • Per Serving 609 calories, 15g fat (of which 4g saturates), 51g carbohydrate, 0.6g salt • Gluten Free • Dairy Free • Easy

250g (9oz) basmati rice
8 × 125g (4oz) tuna steaks
5cm (2in) piece fresh root ginger, peeled and grated
1 tbsp olive oil
100ml (3½fl oz) orange juice
300g (11oz) pak choi, roughly chopped
a small handful of freshly chopped coriander
ground black pepper
lime wedges to garnish

1 Cook the rice according to the pack instructions.

2 Meanwhile, put the tuna steaks in a shallow dish. Add the ginger, oil and orange juice and season well with pepper. Turn the tuna over to coat.

3 Heat a non-stick frying pan until really hot. Add four tuna steaks and half the marinade and cook for 1–2 minutes on each side until just cooked. Repeat with the remaining tuna and marinade. Remove the fish from the pan and keep warm.

4 Add the pak choi to the frying pan and cook for 1–2 minutes until wilted. When the rice is cooked, drain and stir the coriander through it. Serve the tuna with the pak choi, rice and pan juices and garnish with lime wedges.

★ COOK'S TIP
Basmati rice should be washed before cooking to remove excess starch and to give really light, fluffy results.

Special Prawn Fried Rice

Preparation Time 5 minutes • Cooking Time 10–13 minutes • Serves 4 • Per Serving 412 calories, 18g fat (of which 3g saturates), 46g carbohydrate, 1.9g salt • Dairy Free • Easy

- 2 × 250g packs of microwavable rice (see Cook's Tips)
- 1 tbsp sesame oil
- 6 tbsp nasi goreng paste (see Cook's Tips)
- 200g (7oz) green cabbage, shredded
- 250g (9oz) cooked and peeled large prawns
- 2 tbsp light soy sauce
- 1 tbsp sunflower oil
- 2 medium eggs, beaten
- 2 spring onions, thinly sliced
- 1 lime, cut into wedges, to serve

1 Cook the rice according to the pack instructions.

2 Heat the sesame oil in a wok and fry the nasi goreng paste for 1–2 minutes. Add the cabbage and stir-fry for 2–3 minutes. Add the prawns and stir briefly, then add the rice and soy sauce and cook for a further 5 minutes, stirring occasionally.

3 To make the omelette, heat the sunflower oil in a non-stick frying pan (about 25.5cm/10in in diameter) and add the eggs. Swirl around to cover the base of the pan in a thin layer and cook for 2–3 minutes until set.

4 Roll up the omelette and cut it into strips. Serve the rice scattered with the omelette and spring onions and pass round the lime wedges to squeeze over it.

★ COOK'S TIPS

- *If you can't find microwavable rice, use 200g (7oz) long-grain rice, cooked according to the pack instructions – but do not overcook. Rinse in cold water and drain well before you begin the recipe.*
- *Nasi goreng is a spicy Indonesian dish traditionally eaten for breakfast. Nasi goreng paste can be bought at most large supermarkets and Asian food shops.*

Thai Green Shellfish Curry

Preparation Time 10 minutes • Cooking Time 10–15 minutes • Serves 6 • Per Serving 156 calories, 5g fat (of which 1g saturates), 6g carbohydrate, 0.8g salt • Gluten Free • Dairy Free • Easy

1 tbsp vegetable oil

1 lemongrass stalk, trimmed and chopped

2 small red chillies, seeded and chopped (see Cook's Tips, page 42)

a handful of fresh coriander leaves, chopped, plus extra to serve

2 kaffir lime leaves, chopped

1–2 tbsp Thai green curry paste

400ml can coconut milk

450ml (¾ pint) vegetable stock

375g (13oz) queen scallops with corals

250g (9oz) raw tiger prawns, peeled and deveined (see Cook's Tips, page 93), with tails intact

salt and ground black pepper
jasmine rice to serve

1 Heat the oil in a wok or large frying pan. Add the lemongrass, chillies, coriander and lime leaves and stir-fry for 30 seconds. Add the curry paste and fry for 1 minute.

2 Add the coconut milk and stock and bring to the boil, then reduce the heat and simmer for 5–10 minutes until slightly reduced. Season well with salt and pepper.

3 Add the scallops and tiger prawns and bring to the boil, then reduce the heat and simmer gently for 2–3 minutes until cooked.

4 Divide the rice among six bowls and spoon the curry on top. Sprinkle with coriander and serve immediately.

★ TRY SOMETHING DIFFERENT
Use cleaned squid or mussels instead of scallops and prawns.

Thai Noodles with Prawns

Preparation Time 10 minutes • Cooking Time 5 minutes • Serves 4 • Per Serving 343 calories, 11g fat (of which 2g saturates), 40g carbohydrate, 1g salt • Dairy Free • Easy

4–6 tsp **Thai red curry paste**
175g (6oz) **medium egg noodles (wholewheat if possible)**
2 small **red onions, chopped**
1 **lemongrass stalk, trimmed and sliced**
1 fresh **red bird's-eye chilli, seeded and finely chopped (see Cook's Tips, page 42)**
300ml (½ pint) **reduced-fat coconut milk**
400g (14oz) **raw tiger prawns, peeled and deveined (see Cook's Tips, page 93)**
4 tbsp **freshly chopped coriander, plus extra freshly torn coriander to garnish**
salt and **ground black pepper**

1 Pour 2 litres (3½ pints) water into a large pan and bring to the boil. Add the curry paste, noodles, onions, lemongrass, chilli and coconut milk and bring back to the boil.

2 Add the prawns and chopped coriander, reduce the heat and simmer for 2–3 minutes until the prawns turn pink. Season with salt and pepper.

3 To serve, divide the noodles among four large bowls and sprinkle with the torn coriander.

Veggies

Aubergine, Feta and Tomato Stacks

Preparation Time 10 minutes • Cooking Time 12 minutes • Serves 4 • Per Serving 138 calories, 11g fat (of which 5g saturates), 4g carbohydrate, 1.2g salt • Vegetarian • Gluten Free • Easy

200g (7oz) vegetarian feta cheese, crumbled
2 tbsp olive oil, plus extra to brush
1 garlic clove, crushed, plus 1 garlic clove for rubbing
2 plump aubergines, cut into 1cm (½in) thick slices
a handful of fresh basil leaves, torn
3 large vine-ripened tomatoes, each sliced into four
salt and ground black pepper
rocket and toasted ciabatta to serve

1 Preheat the barbecue or grill. Put the feta into a bowl, stir in the oil and garlic, season with salt and pepper and set aside.

2 Brush each aubergine slice with a little oil and barbecue or grill for about 6 minutes, turning occasionally, or until softened and golden. Remove from the heat.

3 Sprinkle a little of the feta mixture on six of the aubergine slices and put some torn basil leaves on top, then a slice of tomato on each. Season well. Repeat with the feta

mixture, basil leaves, aubergine and tomato. Finish with a third aubergine slice and press down firmly.

4 Secure each stack with a cocktail stick. Either use a hinged grill rack, well oiled, or wrap the stacks in foil and barbecue for 2–3 minutes on each side. Serve with rocket leaves and toasted ciabatta rubbed with a garlic clove.

Baked Eggs

Preparation Time 10 minutes • Cooking Time 15 minutes • Serves 2 • Per Serving 238 calories, 21g fat (of which 5g saturates), 2g carbohydrate, 0.6g salt • Vegetarian • Gluten Free • Easy

2 tbsp olive oil
125g (4oz) mushrooms, chopped
225g (8oz) fresh spinach
2 medium eggs
2 tbsp single cream
salt and ground black pepper

1 Preheat the oven to 200°C (180°C fan oven) mark 6. Heat the oil in a large frying pan, add the mushrooms and stir-fry for 30 seconds. Add the spinach and stir-fry until wilted. Season to taste, then divide the mixture between two shallow ovenproof dishes.

2 Carefully break an egg into the centre of each dish, then spoon 1 tbsp single cream over it.

3 Cook in the oven for about 12 minutes or until just set – the eggs will continue to cook a little once they're out of the oven. Grind a little more pepper over the top, if you like, and serve.

Cheese and Vegetable Bake

Preparation Time 15 minutes • Cooking Time 15 minutes • Serves 4 • Per Serving 471 calories, 13g fat (of which 7g saturates), 67g carbohydrate, 0.8g salt • Vegetarian • Easy

250g (9oz) macaroni

1 cauliflower, cut into florets

2 leeks, trimmed and finely chopped

100g (3½oz) frozen peas

crusty bread to serve

FOR THE CHEESE SAUCE

15g (½oz) butter

15g (½oz) plain flour

200ml (7fl oz) skimmed milk

75g (3oz) Parmesan, grated (see Cook's Tips)

2 tsp Dijon mustard

25g (1oz) wholemeal breadcrumbs

salt and ground black pepper

1 Cook the macaroni in a large pan of boiling water for 6 minutes, adding the cauliflower and leeks for the last 4 minutes and the peas for the last 2 minutes.

2 Meanwhile, make the cheese sauce. Melt the butter in a pan and add the flour. Cook for 1–2 minutes, then take off the heat and gradually stir in the milk. Bring to the boil slowly, stirring until the sauce thickens. Stir in 50g (2oz) Parmesan and the mustard. Season with salt and pepper.

3 Preheat the grill to medium. Drain the pasta and vegetables and put back into the pan. Add the cheese sauce and mix well. Spoon into a large shallow 2 litre (3½ pint) ovenproof dish and scatter the remaining Parmesan and the breadcrumbs over the top. Grill for 5 minutes or until golden and crisp. Serve hot with bread.

★ COOK'S TIPS

● *Microwave Cheese Sauce*
Put the butter, flour and milk into a large microwave-proof bowl and whisk together. Cook in a 900W microwave oven on full power for 4 minutes, whisking every minute, until the sauce has thickened. Stir in the cheese until it melts. Stir in the mustard and season to taste.

● *Vegetarian cheeses: some vegetarians prefer to avoid cheeses that have been produced by the traditional method, because this uses animal-derived rennet. Most supermarkets and cheese shops now stock an excellent range of vegetarian cheeses, produced using vegetarian rennet, which comes from plants, such as thistle and mallow, that contain enzymes capable of curdling milk.*

Chickpea and Butternut Pot

Preparation Time 10 minutes • Cooking Time 15–20 minutes • Serves 4 • Per Serving 307 calories, 14g fat (of which 2g saturates), 34g carbohydrate, 2.8g salt • Vegetarian • Gluten Free • Dairy Free • Easy

1 large butternut squash, peeled, seeded and chopped

2 tbsp smooth peanut butter

900ml (1½ pints) hot vegetable stock

2 tbsp olive oil

2 large onions, finely chopped

1 small red chilli, seeded and finely chopped (see Cook's Tips, page 42)

2 tsp mild curry paste (see Cook's Tip, page 72)

225g (8oz) baby sweetcorn

2 x 400g cans chickpeas, drained and rinsed

a handful of freshly chopped coriander

salt and ground black pepper

1 Put the butternut squash, peanut butter and hot stock in a large pan and simmer for 10 minutes until the squash is tender. Remove three-quarters of the squash with a slotted spoon and put to one side. Mash the remaining squash into the liquid, then put the reserved squash back into the pan.

2 Meanwhile, heat the oil in a pan over a low heat and fry the onions, chilli, curry paste and sweetcorn until the onions are soft and caramelised, then tip the contents of the pan into the squash.

3 Add the chickpeas and coriander to the squash and stir through. Season with salt and pepper and cook for 4–5 minutes until piping hot. Serve immediately.

Mushroom Soufflé Omelette

Preparation Time 5 minutes • Cooking Time 7–10 minutes • Serves 1 • Per Serving 440 calories, 42g fat (of which 23g saturates), 2g carbohydrate, 0.6g salt • Vegetarian • Gluten Free • Easy

50g (2oz) small chestnut
  mushrooms, sliced
3 tbsp crème fraîche
2 medium eggs, separated
15g (½oz) butter
5 fresh chives, roughly chopped
salt and ground black pepper

1 Heat a non-stick frying pan for 30 seconds. Add the mushrooms and cook, stirring, for 3 minutes to brown slightly, then stir in the crème fraîche and turn off the heat.

2 Lightly beat the egg yolks in a bowl, add 2 tbsp cold water and season with salt and pepper.

3 In a separate clean, grease-free bowl, whisk the egg whites until stiff but not dry, then gently fold into the egg yolks. Do not over-mix. Heat an 18cm (7in) non-stick frying pan over a medium heat. Add the

butter, then the egg mixture, tilting the pan to cover the base. Cook for 3 minutes or until the underside is golden brown.

4 Meanwhile, preheat the grill. Gently reheat the mushrooms and add the chives. Put the omelette under the grill for 1 minute or until the surface is just firm and puffy. Tip the mushroom mixture on top. Run a spatula around and underneath the omelette to loosen it, then carefully fold it and turn out on to a warmed plate. Serve immediately.

Camembert and Tomato Tarts

Preparation Time 10 minutes • Cooking Time 15–20 minutes • Serves 4 • Per Serving 253 calories, 17g fat (of which 4g saturates), 19g carbohydrate, 1.1g salt • Vegetarian • Easy

½ × 375g pack ready-rolled puff
    pastry
2 tbsp tapenade (see Cook's Tips,
    page 80)
200g (7oz) cherry tomatoes, halved
75g (3oz) Camembert, sliced (see
    Cook's Tips, page 204)

1 Preheat the oven to 220°C (200°C fan oven) mark 7. Cut the puff pastry into four pieces. Put on a baking sheet and cook for 8–10 minutes until risen.

2 Press down the centre of each tart slightly with the back of a fish slice, then spread this area with the tapenade. Top with the tomatoes and sliced Camembert. Put back into the oven for a further 7–8 minutes until golden brown.

Couscous-stuffed Mushrooms

Preparation Time 3 minutes • Cooking Time about 12 minutes • Serves 4 • Per Serving 373 calories, 25g fat (of which 10g saturates), 25g carbohydrate, 0.6g salt • Vegetarian • Easy

125g (4oz) couscous
20g pack fresh flat-leafed parsley, roughly chopped
280g jar mixed antipasti in oil, drained and oil put to one side
8 large flat portabellini mushrooms
25g (1oz) butter
25g (1oz) plain flour
300ml (½ pint) skimmed milk
75g (3oz) mature vegetarian Cheddar, grated, plus extra to sprinkle
green salad to serve

1 Preheat the oven to 220°C (200°C fan oven) mark 7. Put the couscous into a bowl with 200ml (7fl oz) boiling water, the parsley, antipasti and 1 tbsp of the reserved oil. Stir well.

2 Put the mushrooms on a non-stick baking tray and spoon a little of the couscous mixture into the centre of each. Cook in the oven while you make the sauce.

3 Whisk together the butter, flour and milk in a small pan over a high heat until the mixture comes to the boil. Reduce the heat as soon as it starts to thicken, then whisk constantly until smooth. Take the pan off the heat and stir in the cheese.

4 Spoon the sauce over the mushrooms and sprinkle with the remaining cheese. Put back into the oven for a further 7–10 minutes until golden. Serve with a green salad.

Curried Tofu Burgers

Preparation Time 20 minutes • Cooking Time 6–8 minutes • Serves 4 • Per Serving 253 calories, 18g fat (of which 3g saturates), 15g carbohydrate, 0.2g salt • Vegetarian • Dairy Free • Easy

1 tbsp sunflower oil, plus extra
   to fry
1 large carrot, finely grated
1 large onion, finely grated
2 tsp coriander seeds, finely
   crushed (optional)
1 garlic clove, crushed
1 tsp curry paste (see Cook's Tip,
   page 72)
1 tsp tomato purée
225g pack firm tofu
25g (1oz) fresh wholemeal
   breadcrumbs
25g (1oz) mixed nuts, finely
   chopped
plain flour to dust
salt and ground black pepper
rice and green vegetables to serve

1 Heat the oil in a large frying pan. Add the carrot and onion and fry for 3–4 minutes until the vegetables are softened, stirring all the time. Add the coriander seeds, if using, the garlic, curry paste and tomato purée. Increase the heat and cook for 2 minutes, stirring all the time.

2 Put the tofu into a bowl and mash with a potato masher. Stir in the vegetables, breadcrumbs and nuts and season with salt and pepper. Beat thoroughly until the mixture starts to stick together. With floured hands, shape the mixture into eight burgers.

3 Heat some oil in a frying pan and fry the burgers for 3–4 minutes on each side until golden brown. Alternatively, brush lightly with oil and cook under a hot grill for about 3 minutes on each side or until golden brown. Drain on kitchen paper and serve hot, with rice and green vegetables.

Egg Fu Yung

Preparation Time 10 minutes • Cooking Time about 5 minutes • Serves 4 • Per Serving 232 calories, 18g fat (of which 4g saturates), 6g carbohydrate, 0.9g salt • Vegetarian • Dairy Free • Easy

3 tbsp groundnut or vegetable oil

8 spring onions, finely sliced, plus extra spring onion curls to garnish (see Cook's Tip)

125g (4oz) shiitake or oyster mushrooms, sliced

125g (4oz) canned bamboo shoots, drained and chopped

½ green pepper, seeded and finely chopped

125g (4oz) frozen peas, thawed

6 medium eggs, beaten

2 good pinches of chilli powder

1 tbsp light soy sauce

a pinch of salt

1 Heat the oil in a wok or large frying pan, add the spring onions, mushrooms, bamboo shoots, green pepper and peas and stir-fry for 2–3 minutes.

2 Season the eggs with salt and chilli powder. Pour the eggs into the pan and continue to cook, stirring, until the egg mixture is set.

3 Sprinkle with the soy sauce and stir well. Serve immediately, garnished with spring onion curls.

★ COOK'S TIP
To make spring onion curls, trim spring onions into 7.5cm (3in) lengths, shred finely, then place in a bowl of water with ice cubes for 30 minutes.

★ TRY SOMETHING DIFFERENT
This serves four with other dishes as part of a Chinese meal, but for a quick (non-vegetarian) supper for two, add 75g (3oz) cooked peeled prawns.

Polenta with Mixed Mushrooms

Preparation Time 10 minutes • Cooking Time 20 minutes • Serves 6 • Per Serving 383 calories, 13g fat
(of which 4g saturates), 56g carbohydrate, 0.1g salt • Vegetarian • Gluten Free • Easy

50g (2oz) butter

1.1kg (2½lb) mixed mushrooms

1 red chilli, seeded and finely
   chopped (see Cook's Tips,
   page 42)

3 garlic cloves, sliced

100g (3½oz) sun-dried tomatoes,
   roughly chopped

1 tsp freshly chopped thyme, plus
   thyme sprigs to garnish

1kg (2¼lb) ready-made polenta

3 tbsp olive oil

truffle oil (optional)

salt and ground black pepper

1 Melt half the butter in a deep-sided frying pan or wok. Add half the mushrooms and cook over a high heat until all the liquid has evaporated, then set aside. Repeat with the remaining butter and mushrooms. Add the chilli and garlic to the pan and fry for 2 minutes, then add to the mushrooms, together with the sun-dried tomatoes and thyme. Mix well and season with salt and pepper.

2 Slice the polenta into 12 pieces, about 1cm (½in) thick. Heat the oil in a non-stick frying pan. Add the polenta in batches and fry for 3–4 minutes on each side or until golden.

3 To serve, arrange two slices of polenta per person on a plate, top with the mushroom mixture and drizzle with a little truffle oil, if using. Garnish with thyme sprigs.

Spinach and Goat's Cheese Frittata

Preparation Time 10 minutes • Cooking Time 12 minutes • Serves 4 • Per Serving 281 calories, 21g fat (of which 9g saturates), 3g carbohydrate, 0.9g salt • Gluten Free • Easy

200g (7oz) baby leeks, trimmed and chopped
4 spring onions, chopped
125g (4oz) baby leaf spinach
6 large eggs
4 tbsp milk
freshly grated nutmeg
125g (4oz) soft goat's cheese, chopped
1 tbsp olive oil
salt and ground black pepper
mixed salad leaves to serve

1 Preheat the grill to high. Blanch the leeks in a pan of lightly salted boiling water for 2 minutes. Add the spring onions and spinach just before the end of the cooking time. Drain, rinse in cold water and dry on kitchen paper.

2 Whisk together the eggs, milk and nutmeg. Season with salt and pepper. Stir the goat's cheese into the egg mixture with the leeks, spinach and spring onions.

3 Heat the oil in a non-stick frying pan. Pour in the frittata mixture and fry gently for 4–5 minutes, then finish under the hot grill for 4–5 minutes until the top is golden and just firm. Serve with mixed salad.

★ TRY SOMETHING DIFFERENT
Use a different cheese, such as Stilton.

Black-eye Bean Chilli

Preparation Time 10 minutes • Cooking Time 20 minutes • Serves 4 • Per Serving 245 calories, 5g fat (of which 1g saturates), 39g carbohydrate, 1.8g salt • Vegetarian • Easy

1 tbsp olive oil
1 onion, chopped
3 celery sticks, finely chopped
2 × 400g cans black-eye beans, drained and rinsed
2 × 400g cans chopped tomatoes
2 or 3 splashes of Tabasco sauce
3 tbsp freshly chopped coriander
4 warmed tortillas and soured cream to serve

1 Heat the oil in a frying pan. Add the onion and celery and cook for 10 minutes until softened.

2 Add the beans, tomatoes and Tabasco to the pan. Bring to the boil, then reduce the heat and simmer for 10 minutes.

3 Just before serving, stir in the coriander. Spoon the chilli on to the warm tortillas, roll up and serve with soured cream.

⭐ TRY SOMETHING DIFFERENT
Replace half the black-eye beans with red kidney beans.

Spiced Bean and Vegetable Stew

Preparation Time 5 minutes • Cooking Time about 30 minutes • Serves 6 • Per Serving 262 calories, 7g fat (of which 1g saturates), 44g carbohydrate, 1.3g salt • Vegetarian • Gluten Free • Dairy Free • Easy

3 tbsp olive oil

2 small onions, sliced

2 garlic cloves, crushed

1 tbsp sweet paprika

1 small dried red chilli, seeded and finely chopped

700g (1½lb) sweet potatoes, peeled and cubed

700g (1½lb) pumpkin, peeled and cut into chunks

125g (4oz) okra, trimmed

500g (1lb 2oz) passata

400g can haricot or cannellini beans, drained and rinsed

salt and ground black pepper

1 Heat the oil in a large heavy pan over a very gentle heat. Add the onion and garlic and cook for 5 minutes. Stir in the paprika and chilli and cook for a further 2 minutes.

2 Add the sweet potatoes, pumpkin, okra, passata and 900ml (1½ pints) water and season generously with salt and pepper. Cover and bring to the boil, then reduce the heat and simmer for 20 minutes or until the vegetables are tender.

3 Add the haricot or cannellini beans and cook for 3 minutes to warm through. Serve immediately.

Stir-fried Beans with Cherry Tomatoes

Preparation Time 10 minutes • Cooking Time about 8 minutes • Serves 6 • Per Serving 30 calories, 2g fat (of which trace saturates), 3g carbohydrate, 0g salt • Vegetarian • Gluten Free • Dairy Free • Easy

350g (12oz) green beans, trimmed
2 tsp olive oil
1 large garlic clove, crushed
150g (5oz) cherry or baby plum tomatoes, halved
2 tbsp freshly chopped flat-leafed parsley
salt and ground black pepper

1 Cook the beans in lightly salted boiling water for 4–5 minutes, then drain well.

2 Heat the oil in a wok or large frying pan over a high heat. Stir-fry the beans with the garlic and tomatoes for 2–3 minutes until the beans are tender and the tomatoes are just beginning to soften without losing their shape. Season well with salt and pepper, stir in the parsley and serve.

Chickpea and Chilli Stir-fry

Preparation Time 10 minutes • Cooking Time 15–20 minutes • Serves 4 • Per Serving 258 calories, 11g fat (of which 1g saturates), 30g carbohydrate, 1g salt • Vegetarian • Dairy Free • Easy

2 tbsp olive oil
1 tsp ground cumin
1 red onion, sliced
2 garlic cloves, finely chopped
1 red chilli, seeded and finely
   chopped (see Cook's Tips,
   page 42)
2 × 400g cans chickpeas, drained
   and rinsed
400g (14oz) cherry tomatoes
125g (4oz) baby spinach leaves
brown rice or pasta to serve

1 Heat the oil in a wok or large frying pan. Add the cumin and fry for 1–2 minutes. Add the onion and stir-fry for 5–7 minutes.

2 Add the garlic and chilli and stir-fry for 2 minutes.

3 Add the chickpeas to the wok with the tomatoes. Reduce the heat and simmer until the chickpeas are hot. Season with salt and pepper. Add the spinach and cook for 1–2 minutes until the leaves have wilted. Serve with brown rice or pasta.

Summer Vegetable Stir-fry

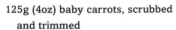

Preparation Time 15 minutes • Cooking Time 7–8 minutes • Serves 4 • Per Serving 78 calories, 4g fat (of which 1g saturates), 7g carbohydrate, trace salt • Vegetarian • Gluten Free • Dairy Free • Easy

125g (4oz) baby carrots, scrubbed and trimmed

1 tbsp sesame seeds

2 tbsp sunflower oil

2 garlic cloves, roughly chopped

125g (4oz) baby courgettes, halved lengthways

1 large yellow pepper, seeded and cut into thick strips

125g (4oz) thin asparagus spears, trimmed

125g (4oz) cherry tomatoes, halved

2 tbsp balsamic or sherry vinegar

1 tsp sesame oil

salt and ground black pepper

1 Blanch the carrots in lightly salted boiling water for 2 minutes, then drain and pat dry.

2 Toast the sesame seeds in a hot dry wok or large frying pan over a medium heat, stirring until they turn golden. Tip on to a plate.

3 Return the wok or frying pan to the heat, add the sunflower oil and heat until it is smoking. Add the garlic to the oil and stir-fry for 20 seconds. Add the carrots, courgettes, yellow pepper and asparagus and stir-fry over a high heat for 1 minute.

4 Add the tomatoes and season to taste with salt and pepper. Stir-fry for 3–4 minutes until the vegetables are just tender. Add the vinegar and sesame oil, toss well and sprinkle with the toasted sesame seeds. Serve immediately.

⭐ TRY SOMETHING DIFFERENT
Vary the vegetables, but always blanch the harder ones first. For a winter vegetable stir-fry, use cauliflower and broccoli florets, carrot sticks, 2–3 sliced spring onions and a little chopped fresh root ginger.

Sweet Chilli Tofu Stir-fry

Preparation Time 5 minutes, plus marinating • Cooking Time 12 minutes • Serves 4 • Per Serving 167 calories, 11g fat (of which 2g saturates), 5g carbohydrate, 1.6g salt • Vegetarian • Dairy Free • Easy

200g (7oz) firm tofu
4 tbsp sweet chilli sauce
2 tbsp light soy sauce
1 tbsp sesame seeds
2 tbsp toasted sesame oil
600g (1lb 5oz) ready-prepared
    mixed stir-fry vegetables, such as
    carrots, broccoli, mangetouts and
    bean sprouts
a handful of pea shoots or young
    salad leaves to garnish
rice to serve

1 Drain the tofu, pat it dry and cut it into large cubes. Put the tofu into a shallow container and pour 1 tbsp sweet chilli sauce and 1 tbsp light soy sauce over it. Cover and marinate for 10 minutes.

2 Meanwhile, toast the sesame seeds in a hot wok or large frying pan until golden. Tip on to a plate.

3 Return the wok or frying pan to the heat and add 1 tbsp sesame oil. Add the marinated tofu and stir-fry for 5 minutes until golden. Remove and set aside.

4 Heat the remaining 1 tbsp oil in the pan, add the vegetables and stir-fry for 3–4 minutes until just tender. Stir in the cooked tofu.

5 Pour the remaining sweet chilli sauce and soy sauce into the pan, toss well and cook for a further minute until heated through. Sprinkle with the toasted sesame seeds and pea shoots or salad leaves, and serve immediately, with rice.

Thai Vegetable Curry

Preparation Time 10 minutes • Cooking Time 15 minutes • Serves 4 • Per Serving 200 calories, 10g fat (of which 2g saturates), 19g carbohydrate, 0.7g salt • Vegetarian • Gluten Free • Dairy Free • Easy

2–3 tbsp red Thai curry paste (see Cook's Tip)
2.5cm (1in) piece fresh root ginger, peeled and finely chopped
50g (2oz) cashew nuts
400ml can coconut milk
3 carrots, cut into thin batons
1 broccoli head, cut into florets
20g (¾ oz) fresh coriander, roughly chopped
zest and juice of 1 lime
2 large handfuls of spinach leaves
basmati rice to serve

1 Put the curry paste into a large pan, add the ginger and cashew nuts and stir-fry over a medium heat for 2–3 minutes.

2 Add the coconut milk, cover and bring to the boil. Stir the carrots into the pan, then reduce the heat and simmer for 5 minutes. Add the broccoli florets and simmer for a further 5 minutes until tender.

3 Stir the coriander and lime zest into the pan with the spinach. Squeeze the lime juice over and serve with basmati rice.

★ TRY SOMETHING DIFFERENT
Replace carrots and / or broccoli with alternative vegetables – try baby sweetcorn, sugarsnap peas or mangetouts and simmer for only 5 minutes until tender.

★ COOK'S TIP
Check the ingredients in the Thai curry paste: some contain shrimp and are therefore not suitable for vegetarians.

Spiced Egg Pilau

Preparation Time 5 minutes • Cooking Time 15 minutes • Serves 4 • Per Serving 331 calories, 9g fat (of which 12g saturates), 50g carbohydrate, 0.6g salt • Vegetarian • Gluten Free • Dairy Free • Easy

200g (7oz) basmati or wild rice
150g (5oz) frozen peas
4 medium eggs
200ml (7fl oz) coconut cream
1 tsp mild curry paste (see Cook's Tip, page 72)
1 tbsp sweet chilli sauce
1 tbsp smooth peanut butter
1 large bunch of fresh coriander, roughly chopped
mini poppadums and mango chutney to serve

1 Put the rice into a pan with 450ml (¾ pint) boiling water over a low heat and cook for 15 minutes or until just tender. Add the peas for the last 5 minutes of cooking time.

2 Meanwhile, put the eggs into a large pan of boiling water, then reduce the heat and simmer for 6 minutes, then drain and shell.

3 Put the coconut cream, curry paste, chilli sauce and peanut butter into a small pan and whisk together. Heat the sauce gently, stirring, without allowing it to boil.

4 Drain the rice and stir in the chopped coriander and 2 tbsp of the sauce.

5 Divide the rice among four bowls. Cut the eggs into halves and serve on the rice, spooning the remaining coconut sauce over the top. Serve with poppadums and chutney.

Asparagus and Mangetouts with Lemon Sauce

Preparation Time 5–10 minutes • Cooking Time 10 minutes • Serves 4 • Per Serving 114 calories, 6g fat (of which 1g saturates), 10g carbohydrate, trace salt • Vegetarian • Dairy Free • Easy

225g (8oz) asparagus spears, trimmed and cut diagonally into three pieces
1 tbsp sesame seeds
1 tbsp vegetable oil
1 tsp sesame oil
225g (8oz) mangetouts
1 garlic clove, crushed
2 tbsp dry sherry
1 tbsp caster sugar
2 tsp light soy sauce
grated zest and juice of 1 lemon
1 tsp cornflour
salt
strips of lemon zest to garnish

1 Cook the asparagus in a pan of lightly salted boiling water for about 5 minutes until just tender. Drain well.

2 Meanwhile, toast the sesame seeds in a hot wok or large frying pan until golden. Tip on to a plate.

3 Return the wok or frying pan to the heat and add the vegetable and sesame oils. Add the mangetouts, garlic and asparagus and stir-fry for 2 minutes.

4 Put the sherry, sugar, soy sauce, lemon zest and juice, cornflour and 5 tbsp water into a bowl and mix well.

5 Pour the mixture into the pan and cook, stirring, until the sauce thickens and coats the vegetables. Sprinkle with the toasted sesame seeds, garnish with lemon zest and serve immediately.

Chickpeas with Spinach

Preparation Time 10 minutes • Cooking Time 12–15 minutes • Serves 6 • Per Serving 204 calories, 10g fat (of which 1g saturates), 21g carbohydrate, 0.8g salt • Vegetarian • Gluten Free • Dairy Free • Easy

3 tbsp olive oil
2.5cm (1in) piece fresh root ginger, peeled and finely chopped
3 garlic cloves, chopped
2 tsp each ground coriander and paprika
1 tsp ground cumin
2 × 400g cans chickpeas, drained and rinsed
4 tomatoes, roughly chopped
a handful of coriander leaves
450g (1lb) fresh spinach
salt and ground black pepper
rice and grated carrots with lemon juice to serve

1 Heat the oil in a large heavy-based pan, add the ginger, garlic and spices and cook for 2 minutes, stirring. Stir in the chickpeas.

2 Add the tomatoes to the pan with the coriander leaves and spinach and cook gently for 10 minutes. Season to taste with salt and pepper and serve immediately, with rice and a salad of grated carrots tossed in a little lemon juice.

Mixed Beans with Lemon Vinaigrette

Preparation Time 15 minutes • Serves 6 • Per Serving 285 calories, 19g fat (of which 3g saturates), 22g carbohydrate, 1g salt • Vegetarian • Gluten Free • Dairy Free • Easy

400g can mixed beans, drained and
    rinsed
400g can chickpeas, drained and
    rinsed
2 shallots, finely chopped
fresh mint sprigs and lemon zest to
    garnish

FOR THE VINAIGRETTE
2 tbsp lemon juice
2 tsp clear honey
8 tbsp extra virgin olive oil
3 tbsp freshly chopped mint
4 tbsp freshly chopped flat-leafed
    parsley
salt and ground black pepper

1 Put the beans and chickpeas into a bowl and add the shallots.

2 To make the vinaigrette, whisk together the lemon juice, honey and salt and pepper to taste. Gradually whisk in the oil and stir in the chopped herbs. Just before serving, pour the dressing over the bean mixture and toss well.

3 Transfer the salad to a serving dish, garnish with mint sprigs and lemon zest and serve immediately.

★ GET AHEAD

To prepare ahead *Complete the recipe to the end of step 2 but don't add the herbs to the vinaigrette. Cover and chill for up to two days.*
To use *Remove from the fridge up to 1 hour before serving, stir in the herbs and complete the recipe.*

Mushrooms with Cashew Nuts

Preparation Time 5 minutes • Cooking Time 5–8 minutes • Serves 4 • Per Serving 75 calories, 6g fat (of which 1g saturates), 2g carbohydrate, 0.1g salt • Vegetarian • Gluten Free • Easy

1 tbsp vegetable oil
25g (1oz) unsalted cashew nuts
225g (8oz) brown-cap mushrooms, sliced
1 tbsp lemon juice
4 tbsp freshly chopped coriander, plus fresh sprigs to garnish
1 tbsp single cream (optional)
salt and ground black pepper

1 Heat the oil in a wok or large frying pan. Add the cashew nuts and cook over a high heat for 2–3 minutes until golden. Add the mushrooms and cook for a further 2–3 minutes until tender, stirring frequently.

2 Stir in the lemon juice and coriander and season to taste with salt and pepper. Heat until bubbling. Remove the pan from the heat and stir in the cream, if using. Adjust the seasoning, if necessary, and serve immediately, garnished with coriander sprigs.

★ TRY SOMETHING DIFFERENT

Chinese Garlic Mushrooms
Replace the nuts with 2 crushed garlic cloves and stir-fry for only 20 seconds before adding the mushrooms. Replace the lemon juice with rice wine or dry sherry.

Pasta with Vegetables, Pinenuts and Pesto

Preparation Time 5 minutes • Cooking Time 15 minutes • Serves 4 • Per Serving 556 calories, 27g fat (of which 6g saturates), 60g carbohydrate, 0.5g salt • Vegetarian • Easy

300g (11oz) penne pasta
50g (2oz) pinenuts
1 tbsp olive oil
1 garlic clove, crushed
250g (9oz) closed-cup mushrooms, sliced
2 courgettes, sliced
250g (9oz) cherry tomatoes
6 tbsp fresh Pesto (see Cook's Tip, page 88)
25g (1oz) Parmesan shavings (see Cook's Tips, pages 50 and 204)

1 Cook the pasta in a large pan of lightly salted boiling water according to the pack instructions.

2 Meanwhile, gently toast the pinenuts in a dry frying pan, tossing them around until golden, then remove from the pan and set aside. Add the oil to the pan, followed by the garlic, mushrooms and courgettes. Add a splash of water to the pan, then cover and cook for 4–5 minutes.

3 Uncover the pan and add the tomatoes, then cook for a further 1–2 minutes.

4 Drain the pasta and return to the pan. Add the vegetables, pinenuts and pesto to the drained pasta. Toss well to combine and serve immediately, topped with the Parmesan shavings.

Fusilli with Chilli and Tomatoes

Preparation Time 10 minutes • Cooking Time 10–15 minutes • Serves 4 • Per Serving 479 calories, 17g fat (of which 4g saturates), 69g carbohydrate, 0.4g salt • Vegetarian • Easy

350g (12oz) fusilli or other short
  pasta
4 tbsp olive oil
1 large red chilli, seeded and finely
  chopped (see Cook's Tips,
  page 42)
1 garlic clove, crushed
500g (1lb 2oz) cherry tomatoes
2 tbsp freshly chopped basil
50g (2oz) Parmesan shavings (see
  Cook's Tips, pages 50 and 204)
salt and ground black pepper

1 Cook the pasta in a large pan of lightly salted boiling water according to the pack instructions. Drain.

2 Meanwhile, heat the oil in a large frying pan over a high heat. Add the chilli and garlic, and cook for 30 seconds. Add the tomato, season with salt and pepper and cook over a high heat for 3 minutes or until the skins begin to split.

3 Add the basil and drained pasta and toss together. Transfer to a serving dish, sprinkle the Parmesan shavings over the top and serve immediately.

Pasta with Goat's Cheese and Sunblush Tomatoes

Preparation Time 5 minutes • Cooking Time 10 minutes • Serves 4 • Per Serving 409 calories, 12g fat (of which 4g saturates), 64g carbohydrate, 0.4g salt • Vegetarian • Easy

300g (11oz) conchiglie pasta
2 tbsp olive oil
1 red pepper, seeded and chopped
1 yellow pepper, seeded and chopped
½ tbsp sun-dried tomato paste
75g (3oz) sunblush tomatoes
75g (3oz) soft goat's cheese
2 tbsp freshly chopped parsley
salt and ground black pepper

1 Cook the pasta in a large pan of lightly salted boiling water according to the pack instructions until al dente.

2 Meanwhile, heat the oil in a pan and fry the red and yellow peppers for 5–7 minutes until softened and just beginning to brown. Add the tomato paste and cook for a further minute. Add a ladleful of pasta cooking water to the pan and simmer for 1–2 minutes to make a sauce.

3 Drain the pasta and return to the pan. Pour the sauce on top, then add the tomatoes, goat's cheese and parsley. Toss together until the cheese begins to melt, then season with pepper and serve.

Pea, Mint and Ricotta Pasta

Preparation Time 5 minutes • Cooking Time 10 minutes • Serves 4 • Per Serving 431 calories, 14g fat (of which 5g saturates), 63g carbohydrate, trace salt • Vegetarian • Easy

300g (11oz) farfalle pasta
200g (7oz) frozen peas
175g (6oz) ricotta cheese (see Cook's Tips, page 204)
3 tbsp freshly chopped mint
2 tbsp extra virgin olive oil
salt and ground black pepper

1 Cook the pasta according to the pack instructions. Add the frozen peas for the last 4 minutes of cooking.

2 Drain the pasta and peas, reserving a ladleful of pasta cooking water, then return to the pan. Stir in the ricotta and mint with the pasta water. Season well, drizzle with the oil and serve at once.

Tomato and Artichoke Pasta

Preparation Time 10 minutes • Cooking Time 10–12 minutes • Serves 4 • Per Serving 380 calories, 11g fat (of which 4g saturates), 59g carbohydrate, 1.3g salt • Vegetarian • Easy

300g (11oz) penne pasta
6 pieces sunblush tomatoes in oil
1 red onion, sliced
about 10 pieces roasted artichoke
    hearts in oil, drained and roughly
    chopped
50g (2oz) pitted black olives,
    roughly chopped
50g (2oz) pecorino cheese, grated
    (see Cook's Tips, page 204)
100g (3½oz) rocket

1 Cook the pasta in a large pan of boiling water according to the pack instructions; do not overcook – it should be al dente. Drain well.

2 Meanwhile, drain the sunblush tomatoes, reserving the oil, and roughly chop. Heat 1 tbsp oil from the tomatoes in a large frying pan, add the onion and fry for 5–6 minutes until softened and turning golden. Add the tomatoes, artichokes and olives to the pan and heat for 3–4 minutes until hot.

3 Add half the cheese and stir in. Remove from the heat and stir in the rocket and pasta. Divide the pasta among four bowls and sprinkle the remaining pecorino over the top to serve.

Very Easy Four-cheese Gnocchi

Preparation Time 3 minutes • Cooking Time 10 minutes • Serves 2 • Per Serving 630 calories, 28g fat
(of which 15g saturates), 77g carbohydrate, 0g salt • Vegetarian • Gluten Free • Easy

350g pack fresh gnocchi
300g tub fresh four-cheese sauce
    (see Cook's Tips, page 204)
240g pack sunblush tomatoes
2 tbsp freshly torn basil leaves, plus
    basil sprigs to garnish
1 tbsp freshly grated Parmesan (see
    Cook's Tips, page 204)
15g (½oz) butter, chopped
salt and ground black pepper
salad to serve

1 Cook the gnocchi in a large pan of lightly salted boiling water according to the pack instructions or until all the gnocchi have floated to the surface. Drain well and put the gnocchi back into the pan.

2 Preheat the grill. Add the four-cheese sauce and tomatoes to the gnocchi and heat gently, stirring, for 2 minutes.

3 Season with salt and pepper, then add the basil and stir again. Spoon into individual heatproof bowls, sprinkle a little Parmesan over each one and dot with butter.

4 Cook under the grill for 3–5 minutes until golden and bubbling. Garnish with basil sprigs and serve with salad.

Pesto Gnocchi

Preparation Time 10 minutes • Cooking Time 10 minutes • Serves 4 • Per Serving 481 calories, 24g fat (of which 6g saturates), 56g carbohydrate, 0.4g salt • Vegetarian • Easy

800g (1lb 12oz) fresh gnocchi
200g (7oz) green beans, trimmed and chopped
125g (4oz) fresh Pesto (see Cook's Tip, page 88)
10 sunblush tomatoes, roughly chopped

1 Cook the gnocchi in a large pan of lightly salted boiling water according to the pack instructions or until all the gnocchi have floated to the surface. Add the beans to the water for the last 3 minutes of cooking time.

2 Drain the gnocchi and beans and put back into the pan. Add the pesto and tomatoes and toss well. Serve immediately.

Tea-time Treats ★

Vanilla Cupcakes

Preparation Time 5 minutes • Cooking Time 15–20 minutes • Makes 12 • Per Cupcake 254 calories, 15g fat (of which 9g saturates), 29g carbohydrate, 0.3g salt • Vegetarian • Easy

125g (4oz) unsalted butter, softened
125g (4oz) golden caster sugar
2 medium eggs
125g (4oz) self-raising flour
1 tbsp vanilla extract
200g (7oz) white chocolate

1 Preheat the oven to 190°C (170°C fan oven) mark 5. Line a bun tin or muffin tin with 12 paper cases.

2 Beat the butter, sugar, eggs, flour and vanilla until smooth and creamy. Half-fill the muffin cases with the mixture and bake for 15–20 minutes until pale golden, risen and springy to the touch. Transfer to a wire rack to cool completely.

3 When the cupcakes are cool, melt the chocolate (see Cook's Tip) and spoon over the cakes, then stand the cakes upright on the wire rack and leave for about 1 hour to set.

 COOK'S TIP
To melt chocolate, break the chocolate into pieces and put into a heatproof bowl set over a pan of gently simmering water, making sure the base of the bowl doesn't touch the water. Heat very gently until the chocolate starts to melt, then stir regularly until completely melted.

Fairy Cakes

Preparation Time 20 minutes • Cooking Time 10–15 minutes, plus cooling and setting • Makes 18 •
Per Cake 160 calories, 6g fat (of which 4g saturates), 26g carbohydrate, 0.2g salt • Vegetarian • Easy

125g (4oz) self-raising flour, sifted
1 tsp baking powder
125g (4oz) caster sugar
125g (4oz) unsalted butter, very soft
2 medium eggs
1 tbsp milk

**FOR THE ICING AND
    DECORATION**
225g (8oz) icing sugar, sifted
assorted food colourings (optional)
sweets, sprinkles or coloured sugar

1 Preheat the oven to 200°C (180°C
fan oven) mark 6. Put paper cases
into 18 of the holes in two bun tins.

2 Put the flour, baking powder,
sugar, butter, eggs and milk into a
mixing bowl and beat with a hand-
held electric whisk for 2 minutes or
until the mixture is pale and very
soft. Half-fill each paper case with
the mixture.

3 Bake for 10–15 minutes until
golden brown. Transfer to a wire
rack to cool completely.

4 Put the icing sugar into a bowl
and gradually blend in 2–3 tbsp warm
water until the icing is fairly stiff, but
spreadable. Add a couple of drops of
food colouring, if you like. When the
cakes are cold, spread the tops with
icing and decorate.

⭐ TRY SOMETHING
DIFFERENT
Chocolate Fairy Cakes
*Replace 2 tbsp of the flour with the same
amount of cocoa powder. Stir 50g (2oz)
chocolate drops, sultanas or chopped
dried apricots into the mixture at the end
of step 1. Complete the recipe.*

Dainty Cupcakes

Preparation Time 15 minutes, plus drying • Cooking Time 15–20 minutes, plus cooling and setting • Makes 12 •
Per Cupcake 306 calories, 14g fat (of which 8g saturates), 46g carbohydrate, 0.4g salt • Vegetarian • Easy

175g (6oz) unsalted butter, softened
175g (6oz) golden caster sugar
3 medium eggs
175g (6oz) self-raising flour, sifted
finely grated zest and juice of
    1 lemon

FOR THE FROSTED FLOWERS
1 medium egg white
6 edible flowers, such as violas
caster sugar to dust

FOR THE ICING
225g (8oz) icing sugar, sifted
1 drop violet food colouring
2–3 tbsp lemon juice, strained

1 Preheat the oven to 190°C (170°C fan oven) mark 5. Line a 12-hole bun tin or muffin tin with paper muffin cases.

2 Put the butter and caster sugar into a bowl and cream together until pale, light and fluffy. Add the eggs, one at a time, and beat together, folding 1 tbsp flour into the mixture if it looks as if it is going to curdle. Fold in the flour, lemon zest and juice and mix well.

3 Spoon the mixture into the cases and bake for 15–20 minutes until pale golden, risen and springy to the touch. Transfer to a wire rack to cool completely.

4 To make the frosted flowers, whisk the egg white in a clean bowl for 30 seconds or until frothy. Brush over the flower petals and put on a wire rack resting on a piece of greaseproof paper. Dust heavily with caster sugar, then leave the flowers to dry.

5 To make the icing, put the icing sugar into a bowl with the violet food colouring. Mix in the lemon juice to make a smooth dropping consistency. Spoon the icing on to the cakes, then decorate with the frosted flowers. Stand the cakes upright on the wire rack and leave for about 1 hour to set.

★ TRY SOMETHING DIFFERENT

Ginger and Orange Cupcakes
Replace the lemon zest and juice with orange and add two pieces of drained and chopped preserved stem ginger. Omit the frosted flowers and make the icing with orange juice instead of lemon. Decorate with finely chopped stem ginger.

Scones

Preparation Time 5 minutes • Cooking Time 15–20 minutes • Makes 12 • Per Scone 124 calories, 5g fat (of which 3g saturates), 18g carbohydrate, 0.3g salt • Vegetarian • Easy

225g (8oz) self-raising flour, plus extra to dust
a pinch of salt
75g (3oz) unsalted butter at room temperature, cut into small pieces
40g (1½oz) golden caster sugar
1 large egg
4–10 tbsp buttermilk or soured milk (milk with lemon juice)

1 Preheat the oven to 220°C (200°C fan oven) mark 7. Sift the flour and salt into a bowl. Add the butter and rub it in until the mixture looks like breadcrumbs. Stir in the sugar.

2 Put the egg into a jug and beat in 2 tbsp buttermilk or soured milk. Make a well in centre of the flour mixture and pour in the egg mixture. Using a round-bladed knife, gradually stir it in. Bring the dough together with your hands – it should be soft but not sticky; if too dry, add a drop more liquid. Shape the dough into a ball and pat into a round.

3 Dust the worksurface and rolling pin with flour, then roll out the dough to a thickness of 2.5cm (1in). Dip a 5cm (2in) cutter in flour, and cut out eight rounds.

4 Arrange the scones on a floured baking sheet. Lightly brush with milk and dust with flour.

5 Bake at the top of the oven for 10–12 minutes until well risen and golden. Cool on a wire rack for 5 minutes before serving.

★ TRY SOMETHING DIFFERENT

Wholemeal Scones
Replace half the white flour with wholemeal flour. Add a little extra milk if needed.

Cheese and Herb Scones
Sift 1 tsp mustard powder with the dry ingredients. Stir in 50g (2oz) finely grated Cheddar, then add the milk. After glazing, sprinkle the tops with a little extra cheese.

Apple Madeleines

Preparation Time 15 minutes • Cooking Time 8–10 minutes, plus cooling • Makes 24 • Per Madeleine 106 calories, 6g fat (of which 4g saturates), 13g carbohydrate, 0.1g salt • Vegetarian • Easy

150g (5oz) unsalted butter, melted and cooled, plus extra to grease
3 large eggs
150g (5oz) caster sugar
1 tsp vanilla extract
150g (5oz) plain flour, sifted
½ tsp baking powder
2 apples such as Cox's Orange Pippins, peeled, cored and finely chopped
icing sugar to dust

1 Preheat the oven to 200°C (180°C fan oven) mark 6. Grease the madeleine tins.

2 Using an electric whisk, beat the eggs and caster sugar together until pale and thick (this should take about 8 minutes), then add the vanilla extract. Quickly but gently, fold in the flour, baking powder and apples, followed by the melted butter, making sure the butter doesn't settle at the bottom of the bowl. Spoon the mixture into the madeleine tins.

3 Bake for 8–10 minutes until golden, then remove from the tins and transfer to wire racks to cool completely. Dust with icing sugar before serving.

Chilled Chocolate Biscuit Cake

Preparation Time 15 minutes, plus chilling • Cooking Time 5 minutes • Cuts into 16 squares • Per Square 206 calories, 12g fat (of which 7g saturates), 22g carbohydrate, 0.4g salt • Vegetarian • Easy

125g (4oz) unsalted butter, chopped, plus extra to grease
150g (5oz) plain chocolate, broken into pieces
250g (9oz) panforte, finely chopped (see Cook's Tip)
100g (3½oz) Italian cantuccini biscuits or Rich Tea biscuits, finely chopped
2–3 tbsp Amaretto, rum or brandy

1 Grease an 18cm (7in) square cake tin and line the base with baking parchment. Put the butter and chocolate into a heatproof bowl set over a pan of gently simmering water, making sure the base of the bowl doesn't touch the water. Stir until melted and set aside.

2 Mix the panforte with the cantuccini or Rich Tea biscuits and the liqueur, rum or brandy. Add the chocolate mixture and stir to coat. Pour the mixture into the cake tin and chill for at least 2 hours. Cut into squares to serve.

★ COOK'S TIP

Panforte is a flat Italian cake, a mixture of dried fruit and nuts, bound with honey and baked on rice paper. It is a Christmas speciality, so look for it in Italian delicatessens and larger supermarkets from November to January.

★ FREEZING TIP

To freeze *Complete the recipe but don't cut into slices. Wrap and freeze for up to three months.*
To use *Thaw at cool room temperature.*

Low-fat Brownies

Preparation Time 10 minutes • Cooking Time 20 minutes, plus cooling • Makes 16 • Per Brownie 172 calories, 8g fat (of which 3g saturates), 24g carbohydrate, 0.1g salt • Vegetarian • Dairy Free • Easy

50ml (2fl oz) sunflower oil, plus extra to grease
250g (9oz) plain chocolate (at least 50% cocoa solids)
4 medium eggs
150g (5oz) light muscovado sugar
1 tsp vanilla extract
75g (3oz) plain flour
¼ tsp baking powder
1 tbsp cocoa powder

1 Preheat the oven to 200°C (180°C fan oven) mark 6. Grease and line a 20.5cm (8in) square shallow tin and baseline with baking parchment.

2 Melt the chocolate in a heatproof bowl set over a pan of gently simmering water, making sure the base of the bowl doesn't touch the water. Remove the bowl from the pan and put to one side to cool slightly.

3 Put the eggs into a large bowl, add the oil, sugar and vanilla extract and whisk together until pale and thick. Sift the flour, baking powder and cocoa powder into the bowl, then carefully pour in the chocolate. Using a large metal spoon, gently fold all the ingredients together – if you fold too roughly, the chocolate will seize up and become unusable.

4 Carefully pour the brownie mixture into the prepared tin and bake for 20 minutes – when cooked, the brownies should still be fudgy inside and the top should be cracked and crispy. Cut into 16 individual brownies immediately, then leave to cool in the tin.

★ TO STORE
Wrap in clingfilm and store in an airtight container. They will keep for up to three days.

Mince Pies

Preparation Time 15 minutes, plus chilling • Cooking Time 12–15 minutes • Makes 24 • Per Pie 150 calories, 8g fat (of which 4g saturates), 17g carbohydrate, 0.2g salt • Vegetarian • Easy

225g (8oz) plain flour, plus extra to
  dust
125g (4oz) unsalted butter, chilled
  and diced
100g (3½oz) cream cheese
1 medium egg yolk
finely grated zest of 1 orange
400g jar mincemeat (see Cook's
  Tips)
1 medium egg, beaten
icing sugar to dust

1 Put the flour into a food processor. Add the butter, cream cheese, egg yolk and orange zest and whiz until the mixture just comes together. Tip the mixture into a large bowl and bring the dough together with your hands. Shape into a ball, wrap in clingfilm and put in the freezer for 5 minutes.

2 Preheat the oven to 220°C (200°C fan oven) mark 7. Cut off about one-third of the pastry dough and set aside. Roll out the remainder on a lightly floured worksurface to 5mm (¼in) thick. Stamp out circles with a 6.5cm (2½in) cutter to make 24 rounds, re-rolling the dough as necessary. Use the pastry circles to line two 12-hole patty tins. Roll out the reserved pastry and use a star cutter to stamp out stars to cover the top of each pie.

3 Put 1 tsp mincemeat into each pastry case, then top with pastry stars. Brush the tops with beaten

egg, then bake for 12–15 minutes until golden. Remove from the tins and leave to cool on a wire rack. Serve warm or cold, dusted with icing sugar.

★ TO STORE

Store in an airtight container. They will keep for up to four days.

★ COOK'S TIPS

● *For vegetarians, make sure you use mincemeat made with vegetable suet rather than beef suet.*
● *Improve the flavour of a jar of bought mincemeat by adding 2 tbsp brandy, the grated zest of 1 lemon and 25g (1oz) chopped pecan nuts. Or, instead of the nuts, try a piece of preserved stem ginger, chopped.*

Blueberry Muffins

Preparation Time 15 minutes • Cooking Time 15 minutes • Makes 12 • Per Muffin 228 calories, 8g fat (of which 3g saturates), 36g carbohydrate, 0.1g salt • Vegetarian • Easy

250g (9oz) wheat-free flour
2 tsp wheat-free baking powder
1 tsp bicarbonate of soda
125g (4oz) golden caster sugar
75g (3oz) ground almonds
finely grated zest of 1 lemon
125g (4oz) dried blueberries
1 medium egg
1 tsp vanilla extract
250ml (9fl oz) skimmed milk
50g (2oz) unsalted butter, melted

1 Preheat the oven to 200°C (180°C fan oven) mark 6. Line a muffin tin with 12 paper muffin cases.

2 Put the flour, baking powder and bicarbonate of soda into a bowl, then stir in the caster sugar, ground almonds, lemon zest and dried blueberries.

3 Put the egg, vanilla extract, milk and butter into a jug and mix together with a fork. Pour this liquid into the dry ingredients and lightly fold together.

4 Spoon the mixture into the muffin cases to three-quarters fill them and bake in the oven for 15 minutes or until the muffins are risen, pale golden and just firm.

5 Transfer the muffins to a wire rack and leave to cool slightly before serving.

★ TRY SOMETHING DIFFERENT
Use chopped dried apricots, dried sour cherries or dried cranberries instead of the blueberries.

Cherry and Almond Muffins

Preparation Time 10 minutes • Cooking Time 25 minutes, plus cooling • Makes 12 • Per Muffin 230 calories, 6g fat (of which 1g saturates), 42g carbohydrate, 0.1g salt • Vegetarian • Easy

225g (8oz) plain flour
1 tsp baking powder
a pinch of salt
75g (3oz) caster sugar
50g (2oz) ground almonds
350g (12oz) glacé cherries, roughly chopped
300ml (½ pint) milk
3 tbsp lemon juice
50ml (2fl oz) sunflower oil or melted butter
1 large egg
1 tsp almond extract
roughly crushed sugar cubes to decorate

1 Preheat the oven to 190°C (170°C fan oven) mark 5. Line a 12-hole bun tin or muffin tin with paper muffin cases.

2 Sift together the flour, baking powder and salt. Add the caster sugar and ground almonds, then stir in the chopped cherries.

3 Whisk together the milk, lemon juice, oil or butter, the egg and almond extract. Pour into the dry ingredients and stir until all the ingredients are just combined – the mixture should be lumpy. Do not over-mix or the muffins will be tough. Spoon the mixture equally into the muffin cases and sprinkle with the crushed sugar cubes.

4 Bake for about 25 minutes or until well risen and golden.

5 Leave the muffins to cool in the tin for 5 minutes, then transfer to a wire rack to cool completely. These muffins are best eaten on the day they are made.

 FREEZING TIP

To freeze *Complete the recipe. Once the muffins are cold, pack, seal and freeze.*
To use *Thaw at cool room temperature.*

Chocolate Banana Muffins

Preparation Time 15 minutes • Cooking Time 20 minutes, plus cooling • Makes 12 • Per Muffin 228 calories, 7g fat (of which 4g saturates), 40g carbohydrate, 0.5g salt • Vegetarian • Easy

275g (10oz) self-raising flour
1 tsp bicarbonate of soda
½ tsp salt
3 large bananas, about 450g (1lb)
125g (4oz) golden caster sugar
1 large egg, beaten
50ml (2fl oz) semi-skimmed milk
75g (3oz) unsalted butter, melted and cooled
50g (2oz) plain chocolate, chopped

1 Preheat the oven to 180°C (160°C fan oven) mark 4. Line a 12-hole bun tin or muffin tin with paper muffin cases.

2 Sift the flour, bicarbonate of soda and salt into a large mixing bowl and put to one side.

3 Peel the bananas and mash with a fork in a bowl. Add the caster sugar, egg, milk and melted butter and mix until well combined. Add this to the flour mixture, with the chopped chocolate. Stir gently, using only a few strokes, until the flour is only just incorporated – do not over-mix. The mixture should be lumpy. Spoon the mixture equally into the paper cases, half-filling them.

4 Bake for 20 minutes or until the muffins are well risen and golden. Transfer to a wire rack to cool completely. Serve warm or cold. These muffins are best eaten on the day they are made.

★ FREEZING TIP
To freeze Complete the recipe. Once the muffins are cold, pack, seal and freeze.
To use Thaw at cool room temperature.

Strawberry and Chocolate Muffins

Preparation Time 5 minutes • Serves 4 • Per Serving 420 calories, 20g fat (of which 12g saturates), 55g carbohydrate, 0.6g salt • Vegetarian • Easy

2 chocolate muffins, halved
4 tbsp mascarpone cheese, softened
600g (1lb 5oz) strawberries, hulled
   and roughly chopped
plain chocolate (at least 70% cocoa
   solids), grated, to decorate

1 Divide the muffin halves among four plates. Top each half with a tablespoon of the mascarpone cheese and a good spoonful of chopped strawberries.

2 Sprinkle with the grated chocolate and serve immediately.

Florentines

Preparation Time 15 minutes • Cooking Time 8–10 minutes, plus cooling • Makes 18 • Per Biscuit 115 calories, 8g fat (of which 4g saturates), 11g carbohydrate, 0.1g salt • Vegetarian • Easy

- 65g (2½oz) unsalted butter, plus extra to grease
- 50g (2oz) golden caster sugar
- 2 tbsp double cream
- 25g (1oz) sunflower seeds
- 20g (¾oz) chopped mixed candied peel
- 20g (¾oz) sultanas
- 25g (1oz) natural glacé cherries, roughly chopped
- 40g (1½oz) flaked almonds, lightly crushed
- 15g (½oz) plain flour
- 125g (4oz) plain chocolate (at least 70% cocoa solids), broken into pieces

1 Preheat the oven to 180°C (160°C fan oven) mark 4. Lightly grease two large baking sheets.

2 Melt the butter in a small heavy-based pan. Add the sugar and heat gently until dissolved, then bring to the boil. Take off the heat and stir in the cream, seeds, peel, sultanas, cherries, almonds and flour. Mix until evenly combined. Put heaped teaspoonfuls on to the prepared baking sheets, spaced well apart to allow for spreading.

3 Bake one sheet at a time, for 6–8 minutes, until the biscuits have spread considerably and the edges are golden brown. Using a large plain metal biscuit cutter, push the edges into the centre to create neat rounds. Bake for a further 2 minutes or until deep golden. Leave on the baking sheet for 2 minutes, then transfer to a wire rack to cool completely.

4 Melt the chocolate in a heatproof bowl set over a pan of gently simmering water, making sure the base of the bowl doesn't touch the water, stirring occasionally. Spread on the underside of each Florentine and mark wavy lines with a fork. Put, chocolate side up, on a sheet of baking parchment and leave to set.

★ COOK'S TIP
Store the Florentines in an airtight container; they will keep for up to two weeks.

Lemon and Nutmeg Shortbreads

Preparation Time 10 minutes • Cooking Time 15 minutes, plus cooling • Makes about 16 • Per Biscuit 114 calories, 7g fat (of which 4g saturates), 13g carbohydrate, 0.2g salt • Vegetarian • Easy

125g (4oz) unsalted butter, softened
75g (3oz) icing sugar, sifted
finely grated zest of 1 lemon
175g (6oz) plain flour, plus extra
    to dust
¼ tsp grated nutmeg
1 egg white, lightly beaten
demerara sugar to sprinkle

1 Preheat the oven to 190°C (170°C fan oven) mark 5. Cream the butter with the icing sugar and lemon zest until pale and fluffy. Sift in the flour and nutmeg, then knead lightly until just smooth.

2 Roll out the dough on a lightly floured surface until about 5mm (¼in) thick. Stamp out rounds, using a 6.5cm (2½in) fluted cutter. Place on baking trays and prick with a fork. Brush with egg white and sprinkle with demerara sugar.

3 Bake for about 15 minutes or until golden. Cool on wire racks.

Millionaire's Shortbread

Preparation Time 10 minutes • Cooking Time 22 minutes, plus cooling • Makes 20 • Per Biscuit 377 calories, 19g fat (of which 12g saturates), 49g carbohydrate, 0.4g salt • Vegetarian • Easy

250g (9oz) plain flour, plus extra
    to dust
75g (3oz) golden caster sugar
175g (6oz) unsalted butter, at room
    temperature, diced

FOR THE CARAMEL
2 × 397g cans sweetened
    condensed milk
100g (3½oz) light muscovado sugar
100g (3½oz) unsalted butter

FOR THE TOPPING
250g (9oz) plain chocolate

1 Preheat the oven to 180°C (160°C fan oven) mark 4. Grease a 30.5 x 20.5cm (12 x 8in) Swiss roll tin and line with greaseproof paper.

2 Put the flour, caster sugar and butter into a food processor and whiz until the mixture forms crumbs, then pulse a little more until it forms a ball. Turn out on to a lightly floured surface and knead to combine.

3 Press into the prepared tin and bake for 20 minutes until firm to the touch and very pale brown.

4 For the caramel, put the condensed milk, muscovado sugar and butter into a heatproof bowl and microwave at full power for 12 minutes (based on a 900W oven), beating with a balloon whisk every 2–3 minutes until the mixture is thick and fudgey. Spoon on to the shortbread and smooth over, then leave to cool.

5 For the topping, put the chocolate into a heatproof bowl and microwave on Medium for 2 minutes until melted. Pour over the caramel and leave to set at room temperature, then cut into 20 squares to serve.

Cherry Chocolate Chip Cookies

Preparation Time 20 minutes • Cooking Time 10–12 minutes, plus cooling • Makes 24 • Per Cookie 104 calories, 5g fat (of which 3g saturates), 15g carbohydrate, 0.1g salt • Vegetarian • Easy

75g (3oz) unsalted butter, softened, plus extra to grease
25g (1oz) caster sugar
50g (2oz) light muscovado sugar
a few drops of vanilla extract
1 large egg, lightly beaten
175g (6oz) self-raising flour, sifted
finely grated zest of 1 orange
125g (4oz) white chocolate, broken into pieces
125g (4oz) glacé cherries, roughly chopped

1 Preheat the oven to 180°C (160°C fan oven) mark 4 and grease several baking sheets. Using a hand-held electric whisk, beat together the butter, caster sugar, muscovado sugar and vanilla extract in a large bowl until well combined. Gradually beat in the egg until the mixture is light and fluffy.

2 Using a large metal spoon, lightly fold in the flour, orange zest, chocolate and glacé cherries. Put heaped teaspoonfuls of the mixture, spaced well apart, on the prepared baking sheets.

3 Press lightly with the back of a spoon and bake for 10–12 minutes. The biscuits should be soft under a crisp crust. Leave on the baking sheets for 1 minute, then transfer to a wire rack to cool completely.

TO STORE

Store in an airtight container. They will keep for up to three days.

Sultana and Pecan Cookies

Preparation Time 15 minutes • Cooking Time 12–15 minutes, plus cooling • Makes 20 • Per Cookie 276 calories, 18g fat (of which 7g saturates), 27g carbohydrate, 0.2g salt • Vegetarian • Easy

225g (8oz) unsalted butter, at room temperature, plus extra to grease
175g (6oz) light muscovado sugar
2 medium eggs, lightly beaten
225g (8oz) pecan nut halves
300g (11oz) self-raising flour, sifted
¼ tsp baking powder
125g (4oz) sultanas
2 tbsp maple syrup

1 Preheat the oven to 190°C (170°C fan oven) mark 5 and grease four baking sheets.

2 Cream together the butter and sugar until the mixture is pale and fluffy. Gradually beat in the eggs until thoroughly combined.

3 Put 20 pecan nut halves to one side, then roughly chop the rest and fold into the mixture with the flour, baking powder, sultanas and maple syrup.

4 Roll the mixture into 20 balls and place them, spaced well apart, on the baking sheets. Flatten the cookies with a dampened palette knife and top each with a piece of pecan nut. Bake for 12–15 minutes until pale golden.

5 Leave on the baking sheets for 5 minutes, then transfer to a wire rack to cool completely.

★ FREEZING TIP
To freeze *Open-freeze a tray of unbaked cookies, then pack into bags or containers and freeze.*
To use *Cook from frozen for 18–20 minutes.*

Almond Cookies

Preparation Time 15 minutes • Cooking Time 15–20 minutes, plus cooling • Makes 12 • Per Cookie 204 calories, 10g fat (of which 1g saturates), 27g carbohydrate, 0g salt • Vegetarian • Dairy Free • Easy

rice paper to line
2 medium egg whites
200g (7oz) caster sugar
200g (7oz) ground almonds
finely grated zest of 1 orange
½ tsp ground ginger
40g (1½oz) stem ginger in syrup, drained and roughly chopped
2 tbsp plain flour, sifted, to dust
12 natural glacé cherries

1 Preheat the oven to 180°C (160°C fan oven) mark 4. Line two baking sheets with rice paper. Put the egg whites into a large, clean, grease-free bowl and whisk until they form stiff peaks. In another large bowl, stir together the sugar, ground almonds, orange zest, ¼ tsp ground ginger and the stem ginger. With a wooden spoon, mix in the egg whites to form a sticky dough.

2 Roll the dough into 12 equal-sized balls. Mix the flour and remaining ground ginger together in a bowl. Lightly coat each ball in the flour and shake off the excess. Put the balls, spaced well apart, on the prepared baking sheets. Using a dampened palette knife, flatten each one into a round.

3 Push a glacé cherry into the middle of each cookie and bake for 15–20 minutes until lightly golden.

4 Cool on a wire rack, then trim away the excess rice paper.

★ TRY SOMETHING DIFFERENT
Instead of a glacé cherry, use whole almonds or a sprinkling of lemon zest to top each cookie.

★ TO STORE
Store in an airtight container. They will keep for up to one week.

Chocolate Crispies

Preparation Time 15 minutes, plus cooling • Makes 40 • Per Crispie 61 calories, 2g fat (of which 1g saturates), 10g carbohydrate, 0.1g salt • Vegetarian • Easy

400g (14oz) Mars Bars, sliced
2 tbsp golden syrup
15g (½oz) butter
12 glacé cherries, diced
50g (2oz) raisins
50g (2oz) Rice Krispies

1 Put the Mars Bars, syrup and butter into a pan and heat gently until the Mars Bars have melted.

2 Add the cherries, raisins and Rice Krispies and mix together quickly. Spoon into a 25.5 x 15cm (10 x 6in) non-stick tin and level the surface. Alternatively, use a 20.5cm (8in) square tin. Leave to set.

3 Turn the mixture out on to a board and cut into small squares.

★ TRY SOMETHING DIFFERENT
Replace the raisins with 50g (2oz) chopped toasted hazelnuts.

Puddings and Desserts

Chocolate and Chestnut Roulade

Preparation Time 20 minutes • Cooking Time 20–25 minutes, plus cooling • Cuts into 10 slices • Per Slice 409 calories, 28g fat (of which 17g saturates), 36g carbohydrate, 0.3g salt • Gluten Free • Easy

a little vegetable oil to grease
6 medium eggs, separated
200g (7oz) caster sugar, plus extra to dust
2–3 drops of vanilla extract
50g (2oz) cocoa powder, sifted

FOR THE FILLING
125g (4oz) plain chocolate (at least 50% cocoa solids), broken into pieces
300ml (½ pint) double cream
225g (8oz) unsweetened chestnut purée
200ml (7fl oz) full-fat crème fraîche
50g (2oz) icing sugar

1 Preheat the oven to 180°C (160°C fan oven) mark 4. Lightly oil a 33 x 20.5cm (13 x 8in) Swiss roll tin, then line with greaseproof paper.

2 Put the egg yolks, caster sugar and vanilla into a large bowl and whisk until pale and thick. Using a large metal spoon, fold in the cocoa powder. Put the egg whites into a clean, grease-free bowl and whisk until stiff peaks form. Fold into the cocoa mixture, then spoon the mixture into the prepared tin.

3 Bake for 20–25 minutes until just cooked – the top should be springy to the touch. Leave to cool in the tin for 10–15 minutes. Dust a sheet of baking parchment with caster sugar. Carefully turn out the roulade on to the parchment, then leave to cool. Peel away the lining paper.

4 Meanwhile, make the filling. Put the chocolate into a heatproof bowl set over a pan of gently simmering water, making sure the base of the bowl doesn't touch the water. Leave to melt. In a separate bowl, lightly whip the cream. Beat the chestnut purée into the chocolate until smooth – the mixture will be quite thick. Whisk in the crème fraîche and icing sugar. Beat 1 tbsp of the whipped cream into the chocolate mixture, then use a metal spoon to fold in half the remaining cream.

5 Spread the filling over the roulade, then spread the remaining cream on top. Roll the roulade up from one of the narrow ends, using the baking parchment to help. Lift on to a serving plate and dust with caster sugar. Serve immediately.

Raspberry Cheesecake

Preparation Time 25 minutes, plus chilling • Cooking Time 5 minutes • Serves 10 • Per Serving 270 calories, 19g fat (of which 10g saturates), 20g carbohydrate, 0.5g salt • Easy

100g (3½oz) unsalted butter, melted, plus extra to grease
25g (1oz) blanched almonds, lightly toasted, then finely chopped
225g (8oz) almond butter biscuits, crushed
a few drops of almond extract
450g (1lb) raspberries
300g (11oz) Greek yogurt
150g (5oz) low-fat soft cheese
1 tbsp powdered gelatine
2 medium egg whites
50g (2oz) icing sugar

1 Grease a 20.5cm (8in) round springform cake tin. Mix the almonds with the crushed biscuits and melted butter, then add the almond extract. Tip the crumb mixture into the prepared tin and press evenly on to the base, using the back of a spoon to level the surface. Chill for 1 hour or until firm.

2 To make the filling, purée 225g (8oz) raspberries in a blender, then press through a sieve. Put three-quarters of the purée to one side and return the rest to the blender. Add the yogurt and cheese, then whiz to blend. Transfer to a bowl. Sprinkle the gelatine over 2 tbsp water in a heatproof bowl and leave to soak for 2–3 minutes. Put the bowl over a pan of simmering water until the gelatine has dissolved.

3 Whisk the egg whites with the icing sugar until thick and shiny. Fold into the cheese mixture. Arrange half the remaining berries over the biscuit base, then pour the cheese mixture over the berries. Add the reserved purée and swirl with a knife to marble. Top with the remaining berries and chill for 3–4 hours.

★ TRY SOMETHING DIFFERENT

Blueberry Cheesecake
Replace the raspberries with blueberries.

Pineapple and Ginger Cheesecake
Omit the almonds and replace the almond biscuits with 250g (9oz) crushed gingernut biscuits. Omit the almond extract. Replace the raspberries with fresh pineapple chunks.

Quick Apple Tart

Preparation Time 10 minutes • Cooking Time 20–25 minutes • Serves 8 • Per Serving 221 calories, 12g fat
(of which 0g saturates), 29g carbohydrate, 0.4g salt • Vegetarian • Easy

**375g packet all-butter ready-rolled
puff pastry
500g (1lb 2oz) Cox's Orange Pippin
apples, cored, thinly sliced and
tossed in the juice of 1 lemon
golden icing sugar to dust**

1 Preheat the oven to 200°C (180°C fan oven) mark 6. Put the pastry on a 28 x 38cm (11 x 15in) baking sheet and roll lightly with a rolling pin to smooth down the pastry. Score lightly around the edge, to create a 3cm (1 ¼ in) border.

2 Put the apple slices on top of the pastry, within the border. Turn the edge of the pastry halfway over, so that it reaches the edge of the apples, then press down and use your fingers to crimp the edge. Dust heavily with icing sugar.

3 Bake in the oven for 20–25 minutes until the pastry is cooked and the sugar has caramelised. Serve warm, dusted with more icing sugar.

Baked Apricots with Almonds

Preparation Time 5 minutes • Cooking Time 20–25 minutes • Serves 6 • Per Serving 124 calories, 6g fat (of which 2g saturates), 16g carbohydrate, 0.1g salt • Vegetarian • Gluten Free • Easy

12 apricots, halved and stoned
3 tbsp golden caster sugar
2 tbsp Amaretto liqueur
25g (1oz) unsalted butter
25g (1oz) flaked almonds
crème fraîche to serve

1 Preheat the oven to 200°C (180°C fan oven) mark 6. Put the apricot halves, cut side up, into an ovenproof dish. Sprinkle with the sugar, drizzle with the liqueur, then dot each apricot half with a little butter. Scatter the flaked almonds over them.

2 Bake in the oven for 20–25 minutes until the apricots are soft and the juices are syrupy. Serve warm, with crème fraîche.

★ TRY SOMETHING DIFFERENT
Use nectarines or peaches instead of apricots.

Ginger-glazed Pineapple

Preparation Time 10 minutes • Cooking Time 10 minutes • Serves 6 • Per Serving 88 calories, trace fat, 22g carbohydrate, 0g salt • Vegetarian • Gluten Free • Dairy Free • Easy

2 pineapples
2 tbsp light muscovado sugar
2 tsp ground ginger
honey and natural yogurt (optional) to serve

1 Cut the pineapples into quarters lengthways, leaving the stalk intact. Remove the core, extract the flesh and reserve the skin. Cut the flesh into pieces and return to the pineapple shell. Wrap the green leaves of the stalk in foil.

2 Preheat the grill. Mix the sugar with the ginger. Sprinkle each pineapple quarter with the sugar mixture. Put on foil-lined baking sheets and grill for 10 minutes until golden and caramelised. Serve with natural yogurt, if you like, and a drizzle of runny honey.

⭐ COOK'S TIP
This is the perfect dessert after a heavy or rich meal. Fresh pineapple contains an enzyme, bromelin, which digests protein very effectively and helps balance any excess acidity or alkalinity. Ginger is a well-known digestive and has many therapeutic properties.

Sticky Maple Syrup Pineapple

Preparation Time 15 minutes • Cooking Time 5 minutes • Serves 4 • Per Serving 231 calories, trace fat, 60g carbohydrate, 0.3g salt • Vegetarian • Gluten Free • Dairy Free • Easy

1 large pineapple
200ml (7fl oz) maple syrup

1 Peel the pineapple and cut into quarters lengthways. Cut away the central woody core from each pineapple quarter. Slice each one lengthways into four to make 16 wedges.

2 Pour the maple syrup into a large non-stick frying pan and heat for 2 minutes. Add the pineapple and fry for 3 minutes, turning once, until warmed through.

3 Divide the pineapple among four plates, drizzle the maple syrup over and around the pineapple and serve immediately.

Griddled Peaches

Preparation Time 15 minutes • Cooking Time 6–8 minutes • Serves 4 • Per Serving 94 calories, 5g fat (of which 1g saturates), 11g carbohydrate, 0g salt • Vegetarian • Gluten Free • Dairy Free • Easy

4 ripe but firm peaches, halved and stoned
1 tbsp maple syrup
1 tsp light olive oil
25g (1oz) pecan nuts, toasted

1 Cut the peaches into thick slices, then put into a bowl with the maple syrup and toss to coat.

2 Heat the oil in a griddle or large frying pan, add the peaches and cook for 3–4 minutes on each side until starting to char and caramelise. Sprinkle with the toasted pecan nuts and serve at once.

⭐ TRY SOMETHING DIFFERENT
Use nectarines instead of peaches, or 8 plump plums.

Peach Brûlée

Preparation Time 10 minutes • Cooking Time about 10 minutes • Serves 4 • Per Serving 137 calories, 6g fat (of which 4g saturates), 21g carbohydrate, 0.1g salt • Vegetarian • Gluten Free • Easy

4 ripe peaches, halved and stoned
8 tsp soft cream cheese
8 tsp golden caster sugar

1 Preheat the grill until very hot. Fill each stone cavity in the fruit with 2 tsp cream cheese, then sprinkle each one with 2 tsp caster sugar.

2 Put the fruit halves on a grill pan, and cook under the very hot grill until the sugar has browned and caramelised to create a brûlée crust. Serve warm.

★ TRY SOMETHING DIFFERENT
Use nectarines instead of peaches.

Mango Gratin with Sabayon

Preparation Time 5 minutes, plus optional resting • Cooking Time 10 minutes • Serves 6 • Per Serving 249 calories, 5g fat (of which 1g saturates), 45g carbohydrate, 0g salt • Vegetarian • Gluten Free • Dairy Free • A Little Effort

3 large ripe mangoes, peeled, stoned and sliced
5 medium egg yolks
6 tbsp golden caster sugar
300ml (½ pint) champagne or sparkling wine
6 tbsp dark muscovado sugar to sprinkle
crisp sweet biscuits to serve

1 Arrange the mangoes in six glasses. Whisk the egg yolks and sugar in a large heatproof bowl over a pan of gently simmering water until the mixture is thick and falls in soft ribbon shapes. Add the champagne or sparkling wine and continue to whisk until the mixture is thick and foamy again. Remove from the heat.

2 Spoon the sabayon over the mangoes, sprinkle with the muscovado sugar, then blow-torch the top to caramelise or leave for 10 minutes to go fudgey. Serve with biscuits.

Poached Plums with Port

Preparation Time 5 minutes • Cooking Time 20 minutes • Serves 4 • Per Serving 97 calories, 0g fat, 23g carbohydrate, 0g salt • Vegetarian • Gluten Free • Dairy Free • Easy

75g (3oz) golden caster sugar
2 tbsp port
6 large plums, halved and stoned
1 cinnamon stick
ice cream to serve (optional)

1 Put the sugar into a pan with 500ml (18fl oz) water. Heat gently until the sugar dissolves. Bring to the boil and simmer rapidly for 2 minutes without stirring.

2 Stir in the port. Add the plums to the pan with the cinnamon stick, and simmer gently for 5–10 minutes until the fruit is tender but still keeping its shape.

3 Remove the plums and put to one side, discarding the cinnamon. Simmer the syrup until it has reduced by two-thirds. Serve the plums warm or cold, drizzled with syrup and with a scoop of vanilla ice cream alongside, if you like.

Pears with Hot Fudge Sauce

Preparation Time 5 minutes • Cooking Time 15 minutes • Serves 4 • Per Serving 301 calories, 16g fat (of which 10g saturates), 40g carbohydrate, 0.4g salt • Vegetarian • Gluten Free • Easy

75g (3oz) butter

1 tbsp golden syrup

75g (3oz) light muscovado sugar

4 tbsp evaporated milk or single or double cream

4 ripe pears, cored, sliced and chilled

1 Melt the butter, syrup, sugar and evaporated milk or cream together over a very low heat. Stir thoroughly until all the sugar has dissolved, then bring the fudge mixture to the boil without any further stirring.

2 Put each pear in a serving dish and pour the hot fudge sauce over it. Serve immediately.

Papaya with Lime Syrup

Preparation Time 10 minutes • Cooking Time 10 minutes • Serves 4 • Per Serving 200 calories, trace fat (of which 0g saturates), 50g carbohydrate, 0g salt • Vegetarian • Gluten Free • Dairy Free • Easy

75g (3oz) golden caster sugar
zest and juice of 2 limes
2 papayas, peeled, halved and
seeds removed

1 Put the sugar into a small pan with 100ml (3½ fl oz) water and the lime zest and juice. Heat gently to dissolve the sugar, then bring to the boil and bubble rapidly for 5 minutes or until the mixture is reduced and syrupy.

2 Cut the papayas into slices and arrange on a large serving plate. Drizzle the lime syrup over them and serve.

★ TRY SOMETHING DIFFERENT
This is just as good with mangoes and orange syrup: use 1 orange instead of 2 limes.

Golden Honey Fruits

Preparation Time 5 minutes • Cooking Time 5–8 minutes • Serves 4 • Per Serving 160 calories, trace fat, 40g carbohydrate, 0g salt • Vegetarian • Gluten Free • Easy

900g (2lb) selection of tropical
    fruit, such as pineapple, mango,
    papaya and banana
3 tbsp runny honey
Greek yogurt to serve
mixed spice to sprinkle

1 Preheat the grill to high.
Peel the fruit as necessary and
cut into wedges.

2 Put the fruit on to a foil-lined grill
pan, drizzle with the honey and
cook under the grill for 5–8 minutes
until caramelised.

3 Serve with the yogurt, sprinkled
with a little mixed spice.

Quick Gooey Chocolate Puddings

Preparation Time 15 minutes • Cooking Time 12–15 minutes • Serves 4 • Per Serving 468 calories, 31g fat (of which 19g saturates), 46g carbohydrate, 0.6g salt • Vegetarian • Easy

100g (3½oz) unsalted butter, plus extra to grease
100g (3½oz) golden caster sugar, plus extra to dust
100g (3½oz) plain chocolate (at least 70% cocoa solids), broken into pieces
2 large eggs
20g (¾oz) plain flour
icing sugar to dust

1 Preheat the oven to 200°C (180°C fan oven) mark 6. Butter four 200ml (7fl oz) ramekins and dust with sugar. Melt the chocolate and butter in a heatproof bowl set over a pan of gently simmering water, making sure the base of the bowl doesn't touch the water. Take the bowl off the pan and leave to cool for 5 minutes.

2 Whisk the eggs, caster sugar and flour together in a bowl until smooth. Fold in the chocolate mixture and pour into the ramekins.

3 Stand the dishes on a baking tray and bake for 12–15 minutes until the puddings are puffed and set on the outside, but still runny inside.

4 Turn out, dust with icing sugar and serve immediately.

Mocha Soufflés

Preparation Time 15 minutes, plus cooling • Cooking Time 12 minutes • Serves 6 • Per Serving 132 calories, 5g fat (of which 2g saturates), 20g carbohydrate, 0.2g salt • Vegetarian • Easy

50g (2oz) plain chocolate (at least 70% cocoa solids), roughly chopped
1 tbsp cornflour
1 tbsp cocoa powder
1–1½ tsp instant coffee granules
4 tbsp golden caster sugar
150ml (¼ pint) skimmed milk
2 medium egg yolks
3 medium egg whites
icing sugar or cocoa powder to dust

1 Preheat the oven to 190°C (170°C fan oven) mark 5 and put a baking sheet inside to heat up.

2 Put the chocolate into a non-stick pan with the cornflour, cocoa powder, coffee granules, 1 tbsp caster sugar and the milk. Warm gently, stirring over a low heat, until the chocolate has melted. Increase the heat and cook, stirring continuously, until the mixture just thickens. Leave to cool a little, then stir in the egg yolks. Cover the surface with a piece of damp greaseproof paper and allow to cool.

3 Put the egg whites into a clean, grease-free bowl and whisk until soft peaks form. Gradually whisk in the remaining caster sugar, a spoonful at a time, until the meringue is stiff but not dry.

4 Stir one-third of the meringue into the cooled chocolate mixture to lighten it, then gently fold in the remainder, using a large metal spoon. Divide the mixture among six 150ml (¼ pint) ramekins or ovenproof tea or coffee cups. Stand them on the hot baking sheet and bake for about 12 minutes or until puffed up.

5 Dust the soufflés with a little icing sugar or cocoa powder and serve immediately.

Chocolate Crêpes with a Boozy Sauce

★

Preparation Time 5 minutes, plus standing · Cooking Time 10–15 minutes · Serves 4 · Per Serving 594 calories, 35g fat (of which 17g saturates), 57g carbohydrate, 0.5g salt · Vegetarian · Easy

100g (3½oz) plain flour, sifted
a pinch of salt
1 medium egg
300ml (½ pint) semi-skimmed milk
sunflower oil for frying
50g (2oz) plain chocolate (at least 70% cocoa solids), roughly chopped
100g (3½oz) unsalted butter
100g (3½oz) light muscovado sugar, plus extra to sprinkle
4 tbsp brandy

1 Put the flour and salt into a bowl, make a well in the centre and add the egg. Use a balloon whisk to mix the egg with a little of the flour, then gradually add the milk to make a smooth batter. Cover and leave to stand for about 20 minutes.

2 Pour the batter into a jug. Heat 1 tsp oil in a 23cm (9in) frying pan, then pour in 100ml (3½fl oz) batter, tilting the pan so that the mixture coats the bottom, and fry for 1–2 minutes until golden underneath. Turn carefully and fry the other side. Tip on to a plate, cover with greaseproof paper and repeat with the remaining batter, using more oil as needed.

3 Divide the chocolate among the crêpes. Fold each crêpe in half, and then in half again.

4 Put the butter and sugar into a heavy-based frying pan over a low heat. Add the brandy and stir. Slide the crêpes into the pan and cook for 3–4 minutes to melt the chocolate. Serve drizzled with sauce and sprinkled with sugar.

★ TRY SOMETHING DIFFERENT
Replace the brandy with Grand Marnier and use orange-flavoured plain chocolate.

Summer Gratin

Preparation Time 15 minutes • Cooking Time 15 minutes • Serves 4 • Per Serving 168 calories, 4g fat
(of which 1g saturates), 27g carbohydrate, 0g salt • Vegetarian • Gluten Free • Dairy Free • Easy

**3 ripe peaches, halved, stoned and
   sliced**
**225g (8oz) wild strawberries or
   raspberries**
**3 tbsp Kirsch or eau de vie de
   Mirabelle**
4 large egg yolks
50g (2oz) caster sugar

1 Put the peach slices into a bowl with the strawberries or raspberries and 2 tbsp Kirsch or eau de vie.

2 Put the egg yolks, sugar, the remaining Kirsch and 2 tbsp water into a heatproof bowl set over a pan of barely simmering water. Whisk for 5–10 minutes until the mixture leaves a trail when the whisk is lifted, and is warm in the centre. Remove from the heat. Preheat the grill.

3 Arrange the fruit in four shallow heatproof dishes and spoon the sauce over them. Cook under the grill for 1–2 minutes or until light golden. Serve immediately.

★ TRY SOMETHING
DIFFERENT
*Use mango slices and blueberries and
replace the Kirsch with Cointreau.*

Zabaglione

Preparation Time 5 minutes • Cooking Time 20 minutes • Serves 4 • Per Serving 193 calories, 6g fat
(of which 2g saturates), 28g carbohydrate, 0g salt • Vegetarian • Gluten Free • Dairy Free • Easy

4 medium egg yolks
100g (3½oz) caster sugar
100ml (3½fl oz) sweet Marsala
    wine

1 Heat a pan of water to boiling point. Put the egg yolks and sugar into a heatproof bowl large enough to rest over the pan without its base touching the water. With the bowl in place, reduce the heat so that the water is just simmering.

2 Using a hand-held electric whisk, whisk the yolks and sugar for 15 minutes until pale, thick and foaming. With the bowl still over the heat, gradually pour in the Marsala, whisking all the time.

3 Pour the zabaglione into four glasses or small coffee cups and serve immediately.

Amaretti with Lemon Mascarpone

Preparation Time 15 minutes • Cooking Time 5 minutes • Serves 4 • Per Serving 180 calories, 8g fat (of which 4g saturates), 28g carbohydrate, 0.4g salt • Vegetarian • Easy

finely sliced zest and juice of
   ¼ lemon (see Cook's Tips)
1 tbsp golden caster sugar, plus
   a little extra to sprinkle
50g (2oz) mascarpone cheese
12 amaretti biscuits

1 Put the lemon juice into a small pan. Add the sugar and dissolve over a low heat. Once the sugar has dissolved, add the lemon zest and cook for 1–2 minutes – it will curl up. Using a slotted spoon, lift out the zest strips and lay them on a sheet of baking parchment, reserving the syrup. Sprinkle the strips with sugar to coat.

2 Beat the mascarpone in a bowl to soften, then stir in the reserved sugar syrup.

3 Put a blob of mascarpone on each amaretti biscuit, then top with a couple of strips of the crystallised lemon peel.

COOK'S TIPS
● To prepare the strips of zest, pare the rind from the lemon, remove any white pith, and finely slice the zest into long strips.
● If you're short of time, buy a packet of crystallised lemon slices and use these to decorate the pudding. Alternatively, decorate each biscuit with a little finely grated lemon zest.

Cheat's Raspberry Ice Cream

Preparation Time 5 minutes • Serves 6 • Per Serving 306 calories, 26g fat (of which 16g saturates), 19g carbohydrate, 0g salt • Vegetarian • Gluten Free • Easy

300g (11oz) frozen raspberries
5–6 tbsp golden icing sugar
300ml (½ pint) extra-thick double cream
summer fruit or wafers to serve

1 Put six ramekins or freezerproof glasses into the freezer to chill. Put the frozen raspberries (don't allow them to thaw first) into a food processor with the icing sugar. Whiz for 3–4 seconds until the raspberries look like large crumbs. Add the cream and whiz again for 10 seconds.

2 Spoon into the ice-cold dishes and serve immediately, or spoon into a small freezerproof container and freeze for 20–30 minutes. Serve with summer fruit or wafers, if you like.

★ COOK'S TIP
Depending on the sweetness of the raspberries, you may need to add a little more icing sugar – taste the mixture before you spoon the ice cream into the dishes.

Cherry Yogurt Crush

Preparation Time 10 minutes, plus chilling • Serves 4 • Per Serving 390 calories, 18g fat (of which 9g saturates), 45g carbohydrate, 0.5g salt • Vegetarian • Easy

**400g can stoned cherries, drained,
  or 450g (1lb) fresh cherries,
  stoned**
500g (1lb 2oz) Greek yogurt
150g (5oz) ratafia biscuits
4 tbsp cherry brandy (optional)

1 Spoon some cherries into the base of each of four 400ml (14fl oz) glasses. Top with a dollop of yogurt, some ratafia biscuits and a drizzle of cherry brandy if you like. Continue layering up each glass until all the ingredients have been used.

2 Chill for 15 minutes–2 hours before serving.

Eton Mess

Preparation Time 10 minutes • Serves 6 • Per Serving 198 calories, 5g fat (of which 3g saturates), 33g carbohydrate, 0.1g salt • Vegetarian • Gluten Free • Easy

200g (7oz) fromage frais, chilled
200g (7oz) low-fat Greek yogurt, chilled
1 tbsp golden caster sugar
2 tbsp strawberry liqueur
6 meringues, roughly crushed
350g (12oz) strawberries, hulled and halved

1 Put the fromage frais and yogurt into a large bowl and stir to combine.

2 Add the sugar, strawberry liqueur, meringues and strawberries. Mix together gently and divide among six dishes.

★ TRY SOMETHING DIFFERENT
Caribbean Crush
Replace the sugar and liqueur with dulce de leche toffee sauce and the strawberries with sliced bananas.

Exotic Fruit Salad

Preparation Time 10 minutes • Serves 4 • Per Serving 187 calories, 1g fat (of which 0g saturates), 47g carbohydrate, 0.1g salt • Vegetarian • Gluten Free • Dairy Free • Easy

2 oranges
1 mango, peeled, stoned and
   chopped
450g (1lb) peeled and diced fresh
   pineapple
200g (7oz) blueberries
½ Charentais melon, cubed
grated zest and juice of 1 lime

1 Using a sharp knife, peel the oranges, remove the pith and cut the flesh into segments. Put into a bowl.

2 Add the mango, pineapple, blueberries and melon to the bowl, then add the lime zest and juice. Gently mix together and serve immediately.

★ TRY SOMETHING DIFFERENT
● Use 2 papayas, peeled, seeded and chopped, instead of the pineapple.
● Mix the seeds of 2 passion fruit with the lime juice before adding to the salad.

Tropical Fruit Pots

Preparation Time 15 minutes • Cooking Time 5 minutes • Serves 8 • Per Serving 192 calories, 1g fat
(of which trace saturates), 45g carbohydrate, 0.1g salt • Vegetarian • Gluten Free • Easy

400g can apricots in fruit juice

2 balls of stem ginger in syrup,
    finely chopped, plus 2 tbsp syrup
    from the jar

½ tsp ground cinnamon

juice of 1 orange

3 oranges, cut into segments

1 mango, peeled, stoned and
    chopped

1 pineapple, peeled, core removed,
    and chopped

450g (1lb) coconut yogurt

3 tbsp lemon curd

3–4 tbsp light muscovado sugar

1 Drain the juice from the apricots into a pan and stir in the syrup from the ginger. Add the chopped stem ginger, the cinnamon and orange juice. Put over a low heat and stir gently. Bring to the boil, then reduce the heat and simmer for 2–3 minutes to make a thick syrup.

2 Roughly chop the apricots and put into a bowl with the segmented oranges, the mango and pineapple. Pour the syrup over the fruit. Divide among eight 300ml (½ pint) glasses or dessert bowls.

3 Beat the yogurt and lemon curd together in a bowl until smooth. Spoon a generous dollop over the fruit and sprinkle with muscovado sugar. Chill if not serving immediately.

★ GET AHEAD

To prepare ahead Complete the recipe to the end of step 2 up to 2 hours before you plan to eat – no need to chill.
To use Complete the recipe.

Spiced Nectarines

Preparation Time 10 minutes, plus cooling • Serves 4 • Per Serving 95 calories, trace fat, 23g carbohydrate, 0g salt • Vegetarian • Gluten Free • Easy

4 tbsp clear honey
2 star anise
1 tbsp lemon juice
4 ripe nectarines or peaches,
 halved and stoned
cream or vanilla ice cream to serve

1 Put the honey, star anise and lemon juice into a heatproof bowl. Stir in 150ml (¼ pint) boiling water and leave until just warm.

2 Add the nectarines or peaches to the warm honey syrup and leave to cool. Serve with cream or vanilla ice cream.

★ TRY SOMETHING DIFFERENT
Use a cinnamon stick instead of the star anise.

Apple and Raspberry Mousse

Preparation Time 10 minutes, plus chilling • Cooking Time 15 minutes • Serves 6 • Per Serving 127 calories, trace fat, 32g carbohydrate, 0g salt • Vegetarian • Gluten Free • Dairy Free • Easy

900g (2lb) cooking apples, peeled, cored and sliced
4 tbsp orange juice
grated zest of 1 lemon
225g (8oz) raspberries
6 tbsp golden caster sugar
1 large egg white
mint sprigs to decorate

1 Put the apples and orange juice into a pan and cook over a low heat, uncovered, for 10 minutes until soft. Add the lemon zest, then use a fork to mash to a purée. Cover and chill for at least 1 hour.

2 Gently heat the raspberries and 2 tbsp sugar in a pan until the juices start to run.

3 Whisk the egg white in a clean, grease-free bowl until stiff, adding the remaining sugar gradually until the mixture forms stiff peaks. Fold into the apple purée.

4 Divide the raspberries and any juice among six glasses, spoon the apple mixture on top and decorate with mint sprigs.

Chocolate-dipped Strawberries

Preparation Time 10 minutes • Cooking Time about 10 minutes • Serves 6 • Per Serving 291 calories, 15g fat (of which 9g saturates), 37g carbohydrate, 0.1g salt • Vegetarian • Gluten Free • Easy

100g (3½oz) milk chocolate, broken into pieces
100g (3½oz) white chocolate, broken into pieces
100g (3½oz) plain chocolate (at least 70% cocoa solids), broken into pieces
700g (1½lb) strawberries

1 Put each type of chocolate side by side in a single heatproof serving bowl, keeping each type as separate as you can.

2 Melt the chocolate over a pan of gently simmering water, making sure the base of the bowl doesn't touch the water. Do not stir – keep the three types of chocolate separate. Holding each strawberry by its stalk, dip it into the chocolate. Arrange the strawberries in a shallow bowl to serve. Alternatively, let everyone dunk the berries in the melted chocolate themselves.

★ TRY SOMETHING DIFFERENT
Turn this into a fun chocolate fondue by offering different fruits for dunking, such as mango, pineapple chunks and raspberries, or even marshmallows. Provide a pile of cocktail sticks for spearing the fruit.